Taste the Islands

UNIVERSITY PRESS OF FLORIDA

Florida A&M University, Tallahassee
Florida Atlantic University, Boca Raton
Florida Gulf Coast University, Ft. Myers
Florida International University, Miami
Florida State University, Tallahassee
New College of Florida, Sarasota
University of Central Florida, Orlando
University of Florida, Gainesville
University of North Florida, Jacksonville
University of South Florida, Tampa
University of West Florida, Pensacola

Taste the Islands

Culinary Adventures in a Caribbean Kitchen

Hugh Sinclair, Cynthia Verna, and Calibe Thompson

University Press of Florida

Gainesville

Tallahassee

Tampa

Boca Raton

Pensacola

Orlando

Miami

Jacksonville

Ft. Myers

Sarasota

Photographs are by David I. Muir unless otherwise noted.

This book may be available in an electronic edition.

25 24 23 22 21 20   6 5 4 3 2 1

Library of Congress Control Number: 2019937343
ISBN 978-0-8130-6616-5

The University Press of Florida is the scholarly publishing agency for the State
University System of Florida, comprising Florida A&M University, Florida
Atlantic University, Florida Gulf Coast University, Florida International
University, Florida State University, New College of Florida, University of
Central Florida, University of Florida, University of North Florida, University
of South Florida, and University of West Florida.

University Press of Florida
2046 NE Waldo Road
Suite 2100
Gainesville, FL 32609
http://upress.ufl.edu

Contents

Introduction

In the words of Bob Marley, "a hungry man is an angry man." Thankfully, when you visit the Caribbean region, you'll most likely find lots of happy people! We're fortunate in many of the islands to rarely want for food, even with environmental and social challenges. Thanks to the climate and landscape, we can eat from trees and from the ground in easily accessible wooded areas; if you're a deft fisherperson, you can catch your dinner in shallow waters; and if you don't mind river shrimp, you don't even need to go all the way to the beach. Although people may be hard pressed on other basics and material goods, food is something folks in the region enjoy sharing.

When you're from the Caribbean, it's easy to take the environmental pleasures that tourists enjoy for granted. Sand in our toes, sea breezes, and sunshine on our faces are privileges we can certainly be grateful for. Other places you visit throughout the world might have beaches and mountains, lakes and waterfalls. What you can't find everywhere else, though, is just the right combination of pimento, scallions, garlic, and thyme for a delicious jerk rub, or the right combination of citrus, pork, and *epis* for a tender, juicy fried pork *griot*. Our food is what those of us who leave the islands often miss the most. It is what brings us back together in mom-and-pop restaurants, how we teach our children our culture, and how we share our culture with others. Along with language, music, and art to varying degrees, it is food that most powerfully defines who we are and maintains our legacies, no matter how far we stray from home.

From shared African, European, Middle Eastern, and Asian ancestries, a fairly consistent flavor palette prevails across the region. Many favor seafood, stews, rice dishes, heavy spices and seasoning, and foods grown in the soil. While similarities are clear, from island to island, the foods we enjoy remain subtly but distinctly different.

The wellspring of inspiration for this cookbook is the *Taste the Islands* television series, in which our mission is to invite viewers to explore the Caribbean through the lens of flavor, whether or not they are ever able to visit in person. Chef Irie and Chef Thia were tasked with theming their recipes based on island cultures. They did so with a very personal—and often elevated—approach to the dishes they crafted.

While sharing a wealth of information on their own home Islands—Jamaica for Chef Irie, and Haiti for Chef Thia—they taught us about other island nations like Trinidad and Tobago, St. Lucia, the Dutch Antilles, and Barbados. They also incorporated cooking techniques and flavor elements they picked up on their own international travels, so you'll see the occasional influence of Italy, Spain, and Thailand in these pages as well.

This journey familiarized us with cultural nuances, far more than we could have learned just from looking at recipes. Those subtle similarities and differences across the islands became points of simple fascination. We learned about herbs like culantro and cilantro (yes, they are different), and that Jamaican rice and peas may or may not be the same thing as Bahamian peas and rice. We learned that Latin American polenta, Barbadian *coucou*, and Virgin Islands *fungi* again are close, but not the same. We now know that Haiti uses tomato paste in just about everything, while Trinidad puts tomato ketchup on just about anything.

We are all proud and possessive of our island traditions. But just as our music has proliferated around the world, we believe that our culinary traditions should as well. Ultimately, our goal as a team has been to reach as many people who want to learn about them as we can.

This collection of recipes is an ode to the Caribbean. It will always be our home, even though we may never live full-time in the islands again. We encourage you to visit the Caribbean as often as you can and to enjoy the local food there, because even though you may follow the recipes we've shared to the letter, the air and the soil will most certainly make the authentic island offerings different and better. Until you can go there, we invite you to visit the place we call home without having to leave your own, by way of these recipes. We hope you find comfort in the selection of dishes we've offered. May they also give vibrancy to *your* plates, and your lives!

1

Appetizers

In Caribbean households, while finger foods and snack items are fairly common, the idea of an appetizer as the start of a multi-course meal is primarily entertained among the affluent. For most people, quick bites such as these are what Jamaicans might call a "stop gap."

Fried snacks called fritters are found on multiple islands, with different key ingredients setting each apart. Most popular throughout the region may be codfish fritters. In Jamaica they are pressed flat and called stamp and go. In Barbados they are denser deep-fried balls called fish cakes. In the Dominican Republic and other Spanish-speaking islands they are made similarly to the Jamaican version and are called *bacalaitos*.

In the Bahamas you'll find fritters made with the meat of the conch shellfish. In Haiti, the popular fritters are called *accra*, and are made with grated malanga root as their base, rather than flour. You can try Chef Thia's version in this chapter. In Puerto Rico, *alcapurria* is a fritter made of a green banana and taro root mixture, stuffed with meat, and deep-fried.

Another very simple, popular take on codfish includes shredding and seasoning the fish and pairing it with crackers, *tostones*, or other light starches. This seasoned codfish mixture is done ceviche-style in Haiti and called *chiquetaille*, lightly stir-fried in Jamaica as pick up saltfish, and in Trinidad as saltfish *buljol*.

Double-fried, pressed, and salted chunks of green plantain are called *tostones* in the Latin countries, and simply fried green plantains elsewhere. You may recognize thin fried chips made of green plantains, green bananas, or breadfruit, especially if you live in an area with a large Latino or West Indian population. You can use Chef Irie's recipe to create any of these options. You may also have heard of fried or baked savory pocket pies of different varieties, including *pate kode* from Haiti, patties from Jamaica, and empanadas from the Latin islands. Chef Thia puts her own spin on a *pate kode* recipe, which can be prepared with meat, vegetables, or codfish.

Enjoy your quick dive into appetizers within these pages! And we encourage you to continue to explore Caribbean stop gaps to add some delicious tropical variety to your snackable culinary repertoire.

Plantain Chips

BY CHEF IRIE

Plantain is a very popular Caribbean ingredient, and plantain chips are a huge snack dish in the region and in overseas communities. You can find them in varying thicknesses, but the chips should always be very crispy and golden brown. Thin strips of plantain are deep-fried in vegetable or canola oil, drained, and seasoned or salted. They may then be served on their own, added to a sandwich to give it crunch, or used as a garnish in an entrée. I also pair them with dip, as they can go with any type of dip that you concoct, such as salsa, avocado, spinach, or the ripe plantain dip I make.

Serves 4 to 6

2 green plantains, peeled

Canola oil for frying

1 tablespoon salt

1 tablespoon black pepper

1. Use a sharp knife or mandoline to carefully slice the plantains into very thin, long strips.
2. Heat the oil in a large frying pan or a deep-fryer over medium-high heat, to a temperature of 350°F.
3. Use tongs to carefully place the plantain strips in the oil, one by one, in small batches to keep them from sticking together. Fry until lightly golden brown.
4. Use tongs to remove the chips and place them on paper towels to drain.
5. Season each batch immediately with a light sprinkle of salt and pepper. Enjoy on their own or with Ripe Plantain Cream Cheese Dip (page 3).

Chef Irie's tip: Try seasoning with a spice blend for a more robust kick. Here's one to consider: cayenne, garlic powder, salt, paprika, and ground cumin.

Photograph by Nicole Hylton Richards.

Ripe Plantain Cream Cheese Dip

BY CHEF IRIE

This dish came about through a stroke of random creative inspiration. I thought that ripe plantains and cream cheese would make a good combination in a dip, and as it turns out, they do! The dip has a dreamy sweetness, with just the right texture to be scooped with plantain chips. I recommend using a food processor rather than a blender if possible; food processors can usually handle more volume, they give you more flexibility to get the consistency you want, and you have less risk of the cream cheese clumping to the blades.

Serves 8 to 10

Canola oil for frying

2 ripe plantains, peeled and sliced into 1-inch chunks

1 cup orange juice

8 ounces cream cheese

½ cup dark Caribbean rum

¼ cup light brown sugar

1 tablespoon ground ginger

1 teaspoon ground cumin

¼ teaspoon black pepper

1 teaspoon salt, or to taste

¼ teaspoon paprika

1. Heat the oil in a large frying pan over medium heat to a temperature of 350°F.

2. In small batches, carefully place the plantain chunks in the oil and fry until lightly golden brown. Remove from the oil and place on paper towels to drain and cool slightly.

3. Add half of the orange juice, the cream cheese, and half of the fried plantains to a food processor or blender and pulse a few times. Add all the remaining ingredients except the paprika and pulse to combine, then puree until smooth.

4. Taste and adjust seasoning if desired, then transfer to a serving bowl. Sprinkle the top with a little paprika, for color. Serve.

Chef Irie's tip: If using a food processor, all ingredients can be added at the same time. Add a little more orange juice and perhaps a little more rum if the consistency is too thick.

Pate Kode (Haitian Fried Meat Pies)

BY CHEF THIA

In Haiti many people in the rural areas, especially students, buy this deep-fried meat-filled pie from street vendors. It's a complete meal in one pocket. *Pate kode* was thought of only as street food in the past, but in recent years, Haitian chefs have been changing that perception by focusing on foods from our roots and celebrating them with updated approaches. My version has a light, thin crust and a flavorful creole-style shredded chicken filling. The patty is golden and crispy on the outside and soft on the inside.

Traditional *pate kode* has boiled eggs mixed in, but I've left them out. Add them if you like, and feel free to experiment with ground beef, codfish, or herring fillings instead of chicken.

Makes 4 to 6 patties

For the Filling

2 tablespoons unsalted butter

1 tablespoon tomato paste

1 teaspoon salt

3 tablespoons evaporated milk

¼ cup minced red bell pepper

¼ cup minced green bell pepper

½ cup finely chopped yellow onion

1 teaspoon red pepper flakes

3 teaspoons Chef Thia's Spice (page 66)

1½ cups shredded cooked chicken breast

1 teaspoon black pepper

For the Dough

2 cups all-purpose flour, plus ½ cup to sprinkle on sticky dough

1 teaspoon salt

1 teaspoon baking powder

4 tablespoons unsalted butter, softened

1 teaspoon Chef Thia's Spice (page 66)

½ to ¾ cup cold water

Vegetable oil for frying

1. Make the filling: Heat the butter in a large frying pan over medium-high heat. When the butter is melted, add the tomato paste, salt, evaporated milk, bell peppers, and onion and sauté for 3 to 5 minutes, until the vegetables are tender.

2. Stir in the red pepper flakes and Chef Thia's Spice, followed by the chicken. Sprinkle the black pepper over the top and continue to cook for 3 to 5 minutes, until heated through.

3. Remove the pan from the heat and allow the sautéed mixture to cool.

4. Make the dough: Put the flour, salt, and baking powder in a medium bowl and stir well. Make a small well in the center of the mixture and add the butter, Chef Thia's Spice, and ½ cup cold water. Stir until a smooth and elastic dough is formed, adding up to ¼ cup more cold water by the tablespoon if it's too dry. Cover the bowl and allow the dough to rest for 15 minutes.

5. On a floured surface, roll the dough out to about ¼ inch thick. Use a sharp knife to cut out rectangles that are 4 by 3 inches.

6. For each dough rectangle, place a little of the sautéed mixture in the center, fold, and pinch the sides closed.

7. Heat the oil in a large frying pan or deep-fryer to 350°F. Fry the patties until golden and crispy, 2 to 3 minutes per side, carefully spooning the hot oil over them as they cook.

8. Remove the patties from the oil and place on paper towels to drain. Serve hot.

Accra (Fritters)

BY CHEF THIA

Accra is a type of fritter made of grated, seasoned, and deep-fried malanga (coco) root. I love garlic, so my *accra* is very garlicky. I use a lot of parsley so that you can enjoy the flavor of the herb, too. It's crispy on the outside and very soft on the inside, almost like a dumpling.

You can eat *accra* as is, or pair it with some kind of legume—my black bean soup, for example. If you can't find malanga, the closest substitution would be yuca, also known as cassava.

Serves 4 to 6

½ bouillon cube

1 tablespoon chopped scallion

1½ cups peeled and grated malanga root

2 tablespoons Chef Thia's Spice (page 66)

¼ teaspoon salt

½ teaspoon red pepper flakes

Canola oil for frying

1. In a large bowl, combine all the ingredients except the oil. Mix well so there are no pockets of salt in the malanga.
2. Heat the oil in a large frying pan over medium-high heat.
3. Test the batter by frying a teaspoon of the mixture until golden brown, cool and drain on paper towels, and taste. If needed, adjust the seasoning by adding more spice, salt, or malanga.
4. Use a spoon to scoop out half-moon shapes of the batter, or form small balls if preferred. Working in batches, carefully drop the batter into the hot oil and fry each side until it is deep golden-brown and crispy, 2 to 3 minutes per side.
5. Remove the fritters from the pan and place them on paper towels to drain. Serve warm.

Grilled Okra with Prosciutto

BY CHEF THIA

In the Caribbean we use a lot of okra, usually cooked into stews or deep-fried. People tend to think that you have to boil okra for a long time, but okra is similar to broccoli in that it doesn't necessarily need to be cooked.

I once accidentally dropped some okra into a bowl of orange juice and decided to let it marinate, to see if it would taste good. I had some prosciutto around so I tried wrapping the okra with it and grilling the ensemble. The okra was tender and not at all slimy. You could taste the citrus, and the prosciutto added salty and smoky flavors. Happy accident!

This finger food can be paired with a fruit salsa, grilled fruit, or a watercress salad. The longer you soak the okra, the better the flavor.

Makes 10 bites

5 whole okra pods

1½ cups orange juice

1 teaspoon black pepper

½ teaspoon kosher salt

5 slices prosciutto, cut in half

2 tablespoons unsalted butter

1. Cut the ends off of the okra pods and cut in half lengthwise. Put the okra halves in a bowl and add the orange juice, pepper, and salt and toss to combine. Allow the okra to marinate for 20 minutes.
2. Wrap each okra half with a strip of prosciutto.
3. Take two wrapped okra halves and two wooden skewers; pierce both wrapped okra halves crossways with the skewers, to resemble the shape of a hash tag or pound sign. Repeat with remaining wrapped okra halves.
4. Heat a grill or grill pan and brush the grates with butter. Grill skewered okra for 3 minutes, flip, and continue to grill for an additional 4 to 5 minutes, until the okra is tender and bright green in color. Serve.

2

Salads and Dressings

Vibrant, *colorful*, and *refreshing* are some of the words that might be used to describe the flavor combinations you'll find on the following pages. Both Chef Irie and Chef Thia shine at taking a dish like salad, which can sometimes be uninspired, and making it an eye-catching and unforgettable part of a meal.

The chefs create unique, visually stunning, unquestionably delicious salads using a variety of peppers, fruits, fresh herbs, and surprising flavor elements. You'll see ingredients like breadfruit, jicama, mango, papaya, and chayote squash—many of which may be in your nearby grocery but are also readily found in your local Latin or Caribbean, Indian, or African market. These recipes also use a number of ingredients that are probably available right now in your refrigerator.

Many of these salads will likely leave a lasting impression on you and your guests. For example, Chef Irie's Chayote Salad is slightly sweet and mildly flavored with a fascinating variety of textures in each bite, while his Pineapple Pepper Slaw is a crunchy, tangy side dish, probably best served in the summer months with burgers or grilled kebabs. Chef Thia's Raw Vegan Salad of chayote, carrots, and pear offers elegant simplicity as a stand-alone entrée.

These aren't recipes you'll find in any typical Caribbean kitchen, or likely in any restaurant, anywhere. The chefs' secrets are out!

Breadfruit Pumpkin Salad

BY CHEF IRIE

I grew up eating breadfruit boiled, mashed, roasted, or fried. I always heard people talking about breadfruit salad and so wanted to make something similar. Here, I pair it with pumpkin for contrasting color and texture. Both flavors play nicely with the selection of spices and seasonings I've used.

The texture of both must be soft, but still firm. It's easy to overcook the pumpkin, so be careful. It needs to be firm enough to not fall apart when you start stirring it together with the other ingredients.

You can substitute butternut squash if you can't find calabaza, but there is no substitute for breadfruit. You could use white sweet potato for a similar color and texture, but the flavor will be different, sweeter.

Serves 4

1 cup coconut milk

3 cups peeled and chopped breadfruit (½-inch cubes)

3 cups peeled and chopped calabaza pumpkin (½-inch cubes)

2 tablespoons canola oil

2 tablespoons honey

2 teaspoons mustard

½ teaspoon salt

½ teaspoon black pepper

1 teaspoon Cajun seasoning

2 teaspoons garlic powder

½ cup chopped fresh cilantro

4 scallions, chopped

¼ cup julienned red onion

½ Scotch bonnet pepper, julienned

Juice of ½ lime

1. Heat the coconut milk in a large saucepan over medium-high heat and bring to a boil. Boil for 5 minutes, then reduce the heat to low. Allow the coconut milk to simmer for 30 to 35 minutes, until it has thickened and reduced by about half. Allow to cool, then transfer to the refrigerator to chill completely.

2. In two separate pots, bring salted water to a boil. Add the breadfruit to one and boil for 15 to 20 minutes, just until tender. Add the calabaza to the other and boil for 10 to 15 minutes, just until tender. Be careful not to overcook. Drain and allow to cool.

3. To the chilled coconut milk, add the oil, honey, mustard, salt, black pepper, Cajun seasoning, and garlic powder and whisk to combine.

4. In a large salad bowl, combine the cooked breadfruit and pumpkin, cilantro, scallions, red onion, and Scotch bonnet pepper. Add the coconut dressing and the lime juice, and gently toss the salad to coat. Serve chilled.

Celery Salad

BY CHEF IRIE

This is a salad with a lot of crunch. Celery is a uniquely flavored vegetable, so I came up with this recipe to showcase it in its raw form. Fresh, vibrant, and fairly easy to make, this salad goes well in a chicken or fish sandwich, on a taco, or with sautéed broccoli for a vegetarian dish. Be sure to cut the celery into small bite-size pieces on the diagonal, for a nicer presentation.

Serves 3 to 4

3 tablespoons fresh lime juice

6 tablespoons canola oil

2 tablespoons honey

½ teaspoon sea salt

¼ teaspoon black pepper

1 teaspoon peeled and julienned fresh ginger

6 small okra pods

3 ribs celery, thinly sliced on the bias

1 pint cherry tomatoes, quartered

1 serrano pepper, thinly sliced

1 Scotch bonnet pepper, julienned

1 cup fresh flat-leaf parsley leaves

1. In a small bowl, whisk together the lime juice, oil, and honey. Add the salt, black pepper, and ginger and whisk again.
2. Cut off the ends of the okra pods and slice them into thin circles. Add the sliced okra to the salad bowl along with the celery, tomatoes, serrano, Scotch bonnet, and parsley. Toss well to coat, then cover and refrigerate for up to 30 minutes. Serve chilled.

Chef Irie's tip: Serve freshly made, within 30 minutes of preparation.

Mango Jicama Salad

BY CHEF IRIE

I love mangoes! This salad combines the sweetness of mango with the neutral taste and crunchy texture of jicama. The jicama absorbs the flavor from the mango, the seasonings, and especially the vinaigrette. Serve solo or with fish, poultry, or even on top of a steak. Jicama can be found in the produce section of many supermarkets.

Serves 4 to 6

2 cups peeled and julienned jicama

½ cup peeled and julienned semi-ripe mango

½ cup julienned red bell pepper

1 jalapeño pepper, minced

½ bunch fresh cilantro

¼ teaspoon red pepper flakes

1½ tablespoons honey

3 tablespoons canola oil

2 tablespoons fresh lime juice

1 tablespoon apple cider vinegar

Pinch of salt, to taste

Pinch of black pepper, to taste

1. In a medium bowl, combine the jicama, mango, bell pepper, and jalapeño. Then add the cilantro and red pepper flakes and toss well.
2. In a small bowl, whisk together the honey, oil, lime juice, vinegar, salt, and black pepper.
3. Pour the dressing over the jicama salad and toss to coat. Allow to marinate at room temperature for 30 minutes, or cover and refrigerate overnight. Serve at room temperature.

Kale Salad

BY CHEF IRIE

I wanted to try my hand at a kale dish since so many health-conscious friends enjoy it. I'd made kale chips and sautéed kale but wanted to see how it would work in a salad. As opposed to lettuce, which breaks down quickly, kale stays firm even with dressing. This salad can be paired with Escoveitch Fish and Coucou; stirred into pasta, quinoa, or risotto; or even put on top of pizza.

Serves 4

For the Salad
4 cups stemmed and chopped kale
2 cups diced or julienned semi-ripe
  mangoes
2 cups blueberries

For the Mango Vinaigrette
Juice of 1 lime
1 cup mango puree
¼ cup canola oil
2 tablespoons Dijon mustard
1 teaspoon red pepper flakes
1 teaspoon salt, or to taste

1. Make the salad: Toss all the ingredients together.
2. Make the mango vinaigrette: Blend the vinaigrette ingredients together and adjust the seasoning to taste after dressing has emulsified.
3. Toss the salad and vinaigrette together and refrigerate for up to 1 hour. Serve cold.

Photograph by Nicole Hylton Richards.

Pineapple Pepper Slaw

BY CHEF IRIE

This is a spin on your typical coleslaw, with fruits instead of traditional components like cabbage and carrots. The pineapple pepper slaw is sweet, tangy, and most of all, crunchy—it's all about the crunchiness with this salad! Try it in a fish sandwich or on a burger, or on the side of a freshly grilled kebab. Just be sure to use pineapple that isn't overripe.

Serves 8

For the Salad

2 cups cubed, fresh pineapple

¼ cup finely julienned red onion

1 cup Anaheim peppers sliced into rings

1 cup Cubanelle peppers sliced into rings

½ cup julienned red or orange bell pepper

½ cup julienned yellow bell pepper

1 serrano pepper, thinly sliced

¼ teaspoon salt

½ teaspoon black pepper

1 cup fresh flat-leaf parsley leaves

For the Citrus Vinaigrette

¼ cup apple cider vinegar

¼ cup orange juice

¼ cup fresh lime juice

2 tablespoons light brown sugar

1½ cups canola oil

½ teaspoon salt

Black pepper to taste

1. Make the salad: Put the pineapple, onion, and peppers into a large bowl. Season lightly with salt and pepper. Add the parsley leaves.

2. Make the citrus vinaigrette: In a medium bowl, combine the vinegar and citrus juices along with the brown sugar and whisk until the sugar is dissolved. Continue whisking and start pouring in the oil in a steady stream. Whisk until combined. Season with salt and pepper.

3. Add some of the dressing to the salad and toss well to mix the ingredients. Adjust the seasoning if needed. Place the salad in the refrigerator to chill for about 15 minutes. Cover and refrigerate the remaining vinaigrette. Serve the salad chilled, with the extra vinaigrette on the side.

Green Papaya Mango Slaw

BY CHEF IRIE

This is my Caribbean-style take on a Thai dish that uses green papaya, carrots, and cilantro. The key to this slaw is to use mangoes and papayas that aren't completely ripe. They should be a little firm and not too sweet. Try as a side with my herb-crusted salmon or eat by itself for a healthy and refreshing snack.

Serves 4

¼ cup canola oil

1½ tablespoons Dijon mustard

Juice of 2 limes

Kosher salt and black pepper

1 semi-ripe mango, julienned

1 semi-ripe papaya, julienned

1 green bell pepper, julienned

1 red bell pepper, julienned

1 small red onion, julienned

1 jalapeño pepper, julienned

½ bunch fresh cilantro, roughly chopped

3 tablespoons brown sugar

1. Whisk the oil, mustard, and lime juice in a small bowl. Season to taste with salt and black pepper.
2. Put all the slaw ingredients in a large bowl and add the mustard dressing.
3. Toss well and adjust the seasoning to taste. Place in the refrigerator to chill before serving.

Red Cabbage Slaw

BY CHEF IRIE

This recipe starts as a coleslaw, but I give it a homemade mango ketchup instead of a mayonnaise base to add that Caribbean flavor. I created this dish to add some crunch and textural interest to my bake and shark, which is a popular Trinidadian fish sandwich, but you can pair it with any type of barbecue, hot dogs, hamburgers, or jerk protein.

Serves 2 to 4

1 cup shredded red cabbage

1 cup shredded green cabbage

⅓ julienned cup red bell pepper

¼ cup julienned red onion

2 tablespoons minced fresh cilantro

2 tablespoons minced fresh flat-leaf parsley

3 tablespoons Mango Ketchup (page 65)

1. In a large salad bowl, combine the red and green cabbage, bell pepper, onion, cilantro, and parsley and toss. Add the Mango Ketchup and toss well to coat.
2. Serve right away as a side dish, or piled over bake and shark.

A Day in the Sun with Maxi Priest

When we started soliciting guests for season 1 of *Taste the Islands*, the celebrities we knew were very supportive of the project, particularly since this would be the first time Caribbean personalities were fronting a national series in this way. We were using our own real Caribbean accents, and showing our community from our perspective, rather than presenting a show from the perspective of visitors interpreting and translating our culture. Producer Calibe Thompson, coming from a career in music and entertainment, tapped her industry connections for high-profile cameos, and many of the people we approached knew of Chef Irie, if they didn't already know him personally.

We were tickled when we heard that singer Maxi Priest had agreed to visit us on set, as none of us had an existing relationship with him. The British Jamaican reggae artist topped the music charts in the '90s with songs like "Close to You," "Set the Night to Music," and "Wild World." His long dreadlocks, broad smile, and caramel-tinted good looks are trademarks that have kept him beloved in the Caribbean community for over twenty years, since his first hit record. So when he walked into the backyard we staged as our outdoor kitchen, everyone was understandably excited, and he was happy to share stories about his travels and how he interacted with food in different places around the world.

Facing page: Maxi Priest. *Above*: Maxi Priest and Chef Irie. Photographs by Nicole Hylton Richards.

Nicole Hylton Richards, Calibe Thompson, Chef Irie, and Maxi Priest (*clockwise from top left*). Photograph by Nicole Hylton Richards.

As a Rastafarian—a believer in a faith that takes a holistic view to maintaining the body and mind—his diet is restricted. He would occasionally enjoy fish or chicken, but his meals were mostly vegetarian. Conversing with Chef Irie, he talked about his travels with music legends like Sly and Robbie, Shaggy, Shabba Ranks, and Roberta Flack. And he talked about the challenges of maintaining a healthy eating regimen while constantly on the move between countries. Salads were his default solution.

Maxi admitted he isn't much of a cook, especially since he grew up around a number of sisters who did most of the food prep in his household. He was eager to learn how to put together something simple, healthy, and robust, even while he was traveling. The recipe needed to be straightforward too—his talents apparently didn't extend to the kitchen! Maxi particularly enjoyed the sweetness of the apricots, the little kick of heat from the Scotch bonnet pepper and chile flakes, and the tartness of the fresh lime juice. Thus was created Chef Irie's Lentil Salad, custom made for reggae crooner Maxi Priest, who lent his warm smile and British charm to the set of *Taste the Islands* on a cool December morning in 2014.

Lentil Salad

BY CHEF IRIE

Lentils are usually part of cooked dishes in our culture—stews, rice and peas, and the like. This dish was meant to show how you can utilize cooked lentils in a quick, easy, healthy salad. The texture should be slightly toothsome, so take care not to overcook them. You can use drained canned beans instead of lentils for quicker preparation.

Lentils absorb any added flavors, so the spices, the herbs, the seasoning, and the sweetness of the dried fruit and sweet potato come together to make an extremely flavorful dish.

You can eat this salad alone, pair it with pork or any other protein, or put it in a wrap with other vegetables.

Serves 4 to 6

For the Salad

2 sweet potatoes

1 cup brown lentils

1 cup red lentils

⅔ cup chopped red bell pepper

¼ cup finely chopped red onion

¼ cup diced dried apricots

⅓ cup minced scallions

¼ cup finely minced fresh flat-leaf parsley

¼ cup finely minced fresh cilantro

2 teaspoons red pepper flakes

1½ teaspoons ground cumin

¼ teaspoon salt, or to taste

¼ teaspoon black pepper, or to taste

For the Dressing

½ Scotch bonnet pepper, seeded and minced

Zest and juice of 2 limes

¼ cup orange juice

½ cup canola oil

1. Start the salad: Preheat the oven to 400°F. Wash the sweet potatoes and pierce each several times with a fork. Wrap the potatoes in foil and bake until tender, about 45 minutes. Allow to cool, then place in the refrigerator for 1 to 2 hours, until chilled.

2. Make the dressing: In a small bowl, combine the Scotch bonnet pepper, lime juice and zest, orange juice, and oil and whisk well to combine. Set aside to allow the flavors to meld.

3. Make the salad: Due to different cooking times, separately rinse and drain the brown and red lentils and pour into two separate saucepans, each with 3 cups water. Place the pans over high heat, bring each to a boil, then reduce the heat to a gentle simmer. Simmer until tender, 15 to 20 minutes for the brown lentils and 5 to 7 minutes for the red. Drain and put the lentils in the refrigerator to chill.

4. When the sweet potatoes and lentils are cool, assemble the salad. Peel the sweet potatoes and dice into ½-inch cubes. In a large salad bowl, combine the sweet potatoes, lentils, bell pepper, red onion, dried apricots, scallions, parsley, and cilantro. Sprinkle on the red pepper flakes, cumin, and salt and pepper to taste and gently toss to combine.

5. Pour half of the dressing over the salad and gently fold until the salad is evenly coated with the dressing, adding more dressing as necessary. Serve chilled or at room temperature.

Chef Irie's tip: Be careful handling Scotch bonnet peppers. Remember not to touch your skin or eyes, as the seeds are extremely hot. Flush with cool water if contact occurs.

Photograph by Nicole Hylton Richards.

Herb Apple Salad

BY CHEF IRIE

The star of this salad is the herbs. Herbs, especially raw, have a freshness and vibrancy that can elevate a dish. The apple component makes it a great pairing for pork (like my Pan-Grilled Jerk Pork Medallions), but it also goes well with lamb, fish, or any other protein.

Serves 2 to 4

For the Salad

1 medium Gala or Granny Smith apple, peeled and julienned

2 tablespoons orange juice

⅓ cup fresh cilantro leaves

⅓ cup fresh mint leaves, chopped

⅓ cup fresh flat-leaf parsley leaves

¼ teaspoon kosher salt

¼ teaspoon black pepper

¼ teaspoon ground coriander

For the Vinaigrette

3 tablespoons tamarind chutney

3 tablespoons canola oil

2 tablespoons fresh lime juice

¼ teaspoon kosher salt

1 tablespoon brown sugar

¼ teaspoon ground coriander

¼ teaspoon ground cinnamon

Method

1. Make the salad: Put the apple in a medium bowl with 2 cups water and the orange juice to prevent oxidation.
2. In a large salad bowl, combine the cilantro, mint, and parsley. Sprinkle with the salt, pepper, and coriander and toss to coat.
3. Make the vinaigrette: In a small bowl, combine all the ingredients and whisk together until emulsified.
4. Drain the apple and add it to the herb mixture, pour the vinaigrette over the salad, and toss to coat. Serve.

Chef Irie's tip: If you are unable to find tamarind chutney, add some extra lime juice to the vinaigrette.

Chayote Salad

BY CHEF IRIE

Chayote is used a lot in the Caribbean, usually boiled, roasted, or added to soups or other dishes. It has a neutral and mild taste, so in a raw salad it does a good job of taking on the flavor profiles of the dressing; this recipe offers a sweet, tangy lemon vinaigrette. If you want to switch it up, try jicama instead, which has a similar texture and flavor.

Serves 6

1 cup peeled and julienned carrots

1 cup peeled and julienned chayote

¼ cup julienned red bell pepper

½ cup fresh cilantro leaves

½ cup fresh flat-leaf parsley leaves

½ cup fresh mint leaves, roughly chopped

2 scallions, thinly sliced on the bias

1 tablespoon Dijon mustard

4 teaspoons brown sugar

2 tablespoons fresh lemon juice

3 tablespoons fresh lime juice

¼ teaspoon red pepper flakes

½ cup canola oil

½ teaspoon salt, or to taste

¼ teaspoon black pepper, or to taste

Method

1. Put all the julienned vegetables and the herbs in a medium mixing bowl. Toss to mix together.

2. In a separate medium bowl, combine the mustard, brown sugar, lemon and lime juices, and red pepper flakes, mixing well with whisk.

3. Add the oil and whisk until the liquids emulsify. Taste to check the seasoning and add salt and pepper to taste.

4. Drizzle small amounts of dressing at a time over the vegetable mixture until coated but not oversaturated. Put the salad in the refrigerator for a few minutes. Serve chilled.

Tomato and Avocado Salad

BY CHEF THIA

I've always loved a good Haitian tomato and avocado salad. The sweetness and acidity from the tomato complements the creaminess and special flavor of the avocado. I've added a little more seasoning to the traditional version to make it my own.

In the islands we use the large green avocados, which are creamier and have a different texture than the small, black ones. I recommend this kind if you can find them. Do be sure to use avocados that are ripe but not too soft, and tomatoes that are a touch underripe as well. The tomatoes should be pink and firm, not watery.

Serves 4

½ large avocado

½ cup cherry tomatoes

⅔ cup finely chopped red onion

2 tablespoons chopped fresh flat-leaf parsley

3 tablespoons fresh lemon juice

¼ teaspoon salt

¼ teaspoon black pepper

1. Cut the avocado into quarters lengthwise. Make a small cut on one end of each slice and peel off the skin. Cut each slice into ½-inch chunks and place in a large salad bowl.

2. Cut the tomatoes into quarters. Add to the bowl with the avocado.

3. Add the onion and parsley, drizzle the lemon juice over the mixture, and season with salt and pepper. Gently toss and serve.

Chef Thia's tip: Acidity from the lemon juice will help to prevent oxidation of the avocado.

Raw Vegan Salad

BY CHEF THIA

This recipe landed me my internship at the Ritz-Carlton over hundreds of other applicants. They gave me a mystery basket with one pear, one chayote, one carrot, and some other things, and I had to come up with a dish, so I made this raw vegan salad. It's elegant, crunchy, and fresh with thin grated vegetables and a simple honey-and-lime dressing.

If you can't find chayote, I recommend jicama as a substitute.

Serves 4

1 cup peeled, coarsely grated Bosc pear

½ cup peeled and coarsely grated carrot

1 cup peeled and coarsely grated chayote

2 tablespoons fresh lime juice

⅛ teaspoon salt

⅛ teaspoon black pepper

1 tablespoon honey

1 tablespoon chopped fresh mint

Method

1. Combine the pear, carrot, and chayote in a medium bowl and mix.
2. Add the lime juice and toss.
3. Season the salad with salt and pepper, then mix in the honey and mint.
4. Put in the refrigerator to chill for 1 to 2 hours. Serve cold.

Chef Thia's tip: To prevent peeled pear from turning brown, rub with fresh lime.

Spicy Corn Salad

BY CHEF THIA

Corn is a popular ingredient throughout the Caribbean. In this recipe I combine corn with other common regional ingredients for a dish that is anything but common. This colorful salad is warm and spicy, and bursting with rich flavor in each bite. As a mom I like unfussy, quick, and budget-friendly cooking, and this recipe definitely fits the bill.

I like to pair this salad with roasted chicken and potatoes. If you want to make it extra spicy, use Scotch bonnet pepper instead of jalapeño.

Serves 6 to 8

3 cups organic frozen corn kernels

1 cup diced red onion

¼ cup diced red bell pepper

¼ cup diced yellow bell pepper

¼ cup diced orange bell pepper

1 heaping cup diced jalapeño peppers

2 tablespoons olive oil

½ teaspoon salt

1 teaspoon black pepper

½ tablespoon fresh lemon juice

½ tablespoon chopped fresh flat-leaf parsley

1. Preheat the oven to 350°F.
2. Mix all ingredients together in a large mixing bowl, then spread onto a baking pan.
3. Bake until golden brown, about 15 minutes.
4. Carefully remove from the oven and allow to cool for a minute or two. Serve warm.

3

Soups and Sauces

A good soup warms not just the belly but also the soul. You could say that traditional Caribbean soups include a healthy dose of soul as a necessary ingredient. In the Caribbean, soup can be served as the opening to a meal, but often is hearty enough to be eaten as a meal all on its own.

Regardless of which island you visit, calabaza pumpkin or some variety of legume—frequently kidney bean, black bean, or pigeon pea—is likely used as the base for soups. These ingredients are often paired with vegetables like carrots, chayote, and corn; ground provisions like cassava, Caribbean yellow or white yams, Caribbean sweet potatoes (*boniatos*), plantains, and green bananas give the soups a lot more "body" due to their starch content. Caribbean soups also often include hefty portions of meat, such as beef, pork, chicken, fish, seafood, or even goat. The variety of ingredients, which are bite-sized but which you could potentially eat with a fork, make it easy to see why these soups are akin to complete meals.

We've included some modified versions of traditional soups—for example, Chef Thia's Haitian Black Bean Soup and Chef Irie's Trinidadian Cilantro Corn Soup. We've also reinterpreted some of the usual ingredients to create unique options like Chef Irie's Coconut Pumpkin Rum Soup. Any of these recipes can be made vegetarian by simply omitting the meats.

In the second portion of this chapter, the selection of sauces reflects origins from the islands as well as global influences. Chadon Beni Sauce, for example, is purely Trinidadian, just like the spicy Sauce Chien is purely French West Indian. The sauce paired with the Latin Caribbean–inspired picadillo meatballs is reminiscent of Italy because of its tomato base, but merges into the realm of island cuisine with the addition of dark rum. Chutneys originate in the East, from countries like India and Thailand, but are very popular in Indo-Caribbean communities like Trinidad and Guyana, and have been transformed in those islands by the use of local ingredients. Salsas are traditional to Spanish and European countries, and have been adapted to the Latin Caribbean islands with the use of tropical fruit like pineapple and mango.

Please enjoy the variety of soups and sauces included in these pages, and incorporate local ingredients to make them your own if you like. *Bon mange* (eat well)!

Coconut Pumpkin Rum Soup

BY CHEF IRIE

This velvety soup is flavored with spices like cinnamon, nutmeg, and cloves—
very complex and very delicious.

Serves 6 to 8

¼ cup olive oil

½ cup chopped onion

2 tablespoons finely diced garlic

¼ cup diced green bell pepper

8 cups peeled and diced calabaza
   pumpkin

½ cup brown sugar

1 teaspoon grated nutmeg

1 teaspoon ground cinnamon

1 tablespoon ground ginger

1½ cups dark Caribbean rum

4 cups chicken or vegetable stock

1 tablespoon fresh thyme leaves (no stems)

1 (14-ounce) can coconut milk

1½ tablespoons salt, or to taste

1 teaspoon black pepper

1 whole uncut Scotch bonnet pepper
   (optional)

1. Heat the oil and sauté the onion and garlic for about 2 minutes.
2. Add the bell pepper, calabaza, brown sugar, nutmeg, cinnamon, and ginger
   and sauté until the sugar just starts to caramelize, then add the rum. Let
   cook for another 2 minutes.
3. Add the stock and thyme and cook for about 10 minutes, then remove from
   the heat and puree until smooth using a hand blender.
4. Return to heat and add the coconut milk, salt, and pepper. For an added
   kick, add the whole Scotch bonnet. Stir and let simmer for about 5 minutes,
   then check for seasoning. Serve hot.

Chef Irie's tip: Substitute butternut squash if calabaza pumpkin is unavailable.

Photograph by Nicole Hylton Richards.

Shrimp Chowder

BY CHEF IRIE

This shrimp chowder is a lighter, creamier soup than we normally make, and very chunky. The addition of the smoked bacon adds a nicely balanced, mellow saltiness to the seafood flavor. You can personalize as you like, replacing the shrimp with firm white fish, chicken, even sausage or pork. I would pair this chowder with toasted bread, toasted roti slices, or fried roasted breadfruit.

Serves 2 to 4

10 to 15 large raw shrimp, peeled and deveined

2½ teaspoons kosher salt

1 teaspoon black pepper

¼ cup canola oil

⅔ cup diced smoked bacon

¼ cup flour

2 tablespoons diced red onion

1 tablespoon minced fresh ginger

½ Scotch bonnet pepper, finely diced

3 cloves garlic, minced

4 sprigs fresh thyme

1 tablespoon Jamaican curry powder

½ cup diced carrot

⅓ cup whole kernel corn

¼ cup diced red bell peppers

¼ cup diced green bell peppers

4 cups vegetable or chicken stock

½ cup heavy cream

¼ cup coconut milk

6 large fresh basil leaves, ripped

2 teaspoons chopped fresh flat-leaf parsley

1. Season the shrimp with 1 teaspoon of the salt and the black pepper and refrigerate for at least 30 minutes.

2. Heat the oil in large saucepan over medium-high heat. Render the bacon until crispy. Add the flour and stir for 2 minutes. Add the onion, ginger, Scotch bonnet, garlic, and thyme and sauté for 2 minutes, or until the onion is translucent.

3. Add the curry powder, carrot, corn, and bell peppers and stir until heated through, about 2 minutes.

4. Stir in the stock and the remaining 1½ teaspoons salt, cover, and bring to a boil. Reduce the heat to medium and simmer for 15 minutes.

5. Add the cream and coconut milk and heat for another 10 minutes. Reduce the heat to low, add the shrimp and basil, and gently simmer for about 10 more minutes, until the shrimp has turned bright pink and opaque. Add the parsley and stir.

6. Check for seasoning and add salt if necessary, then remove from the heat. Remove the thyme stems before serving.

Chef Irie's tip: When adding the shrimp, save the shells to use in the base of a seafood stock.

Bacchanal Time

During season 2, we did some filming in Barbados, and our visit to the isle of "Bim" (as the locals call it) started off with a bang.

The first day of activity found us at the Mount Gay Distillery, which is the oldest documented rum factory in the world. *Taste the Islands* host Lisa Lee Arneaud and Mount Gay brand ambassador Dario Prescod chatted on camera about the manufacturing process: how sugarcane juice is reduced into molasses, then fermented using the island's naturally occurring coral-filtered water; how the resulting liquid is single- or double-distilled using copper pot stills to develop Mount Gay Rum's unique taste; and how the distillates are then aged in charred Kentucky white oak bourbon barrels to develop the color in the darker rums. We had the pleasure of sampling a selection of their spirits, both pure and blended, and they were heavenly.

As a rule, the planning of a good Caribbean party, or bacchanal, must include the availability of lots of rum. Accordingly, a proper carnival-related celebration necessarily concludes with the consumption of hot corn soup to counteract the resulting buzz. We got a deeper understanding of the various culinary traditions of bacchanal when we met up with soca queen Alison Hinds. As one of the most respected female voices in soca—the music of Caribbean carnival—Alison shared great insight into the role of traditional eats in carnival culture.

Carnival in Barbados is called Crop Over, so named because the celebrations originally began at the time of the sugarcane harvest, when the work of bringing in the crop was over. At both Barbados's Crop Over and Trinidad's carnival—the mecca of all Caribbean carnivals—it's all about street food like macaroni pie, barbecued pigs' tails, and grilled and fried fish. As Alison spoke, we enjoyed the smells of all those dishes and more being prepared at Bay Tavern, the roadside eatery near the beach where we recorded the interview.

Carnival time is also all about the lime, but not the kind you expect. *Lime* is a verb in Caribbean cultures that means to hang out, chill, lay back, relax, and enjoy yourself. During carnival season, you lime with friends, enjoying many delicious local street food options!

The climax of carnival season and the ultimate bacchanal is the road march—a day of revelry, excess, and fantastic debauchery. At the end of all the drinking and partying, however, revelers come down from the adrenaline rush of the feathers, glitter, drinks, and loud music with a warming cup of corn soup. As Poseidon watched over us from the sea and the sun went down on a lovely day in Barbados, Alison reminisced on the comfort of corn soup as an ideal food to soothe the island reveler's soul. 🔅

Facing page: Lisa Lee Arneaud, Adam Heim, and Tyler Council (*left to right*). Photograph by Lisa Lee Arneaud.
Above: Dario Prescod and Lisa Lee Arneaud. Photograph by Calibe Thompson.
Bottom: Alison Hinds, Calibe Thompson, and Lisa Lee Arneaud (*left to right*). Photograph by Tyler Council.

Cilantro Corn Soup

BY CHEF IRIE

Corn soup is a very popular dish in Trinidad all year round, but especially during carnival time. Trinidadians think of it as comfort food. My version is loosely based on their corn soup, but with fewer vegetables and pureed for a smoother texture. It also has some sweetness and spiciness, and a little tang from the cilantro.

I'd serve this soup with a nice crusty, rustic-style toasted bread. It doesn't need much.

Serves 12

4 fresh ears of corn

¼ cup olive or canola oil

¾ cup chopped onion

4 garlic cloves, chopped

1 tablespoon chopped fresh ginger

Salt and black pepper

½ cup diced green bell pepper

1 cup diced celery

2 cups peeled and diced calabaza
    pumpkin

2 cups yellow split peas

½ cup diced carrot

1½ cups cooked garbanzo beans

1 teaspoon ground cumin

1 teaspoon red pepper flakes

2 sprigs fresh thyme

2 tablespoons chopped fresh cilantro,
    plus sprigs for garnish

12 cups unsalted chicken stock,
    vegetable stock, or water

1. Remove the corn kernels from two ears and save the cobs. Cut the remaining two ears into 1- to 2-inch pieces.

2. In a soup pot, heat the oil and sauté the onion, garlic, and ginger for about 2 minutes over medium heat. Season lightly with salt and black pepper.

3. Add the bell pepper, celery, calabaza, split peas, carrot, and garbanzo beans, stir, and cook for 2 to 3 minutes, then add the corn kernels, pieces of corn, and the cobs to the pot.

4. Add the cumin, red pepper flakes, thyme, and cilantro, then add the stock. Stir well and allow to come to a boil, then reduce to a simmer. Cook for 45 minutes. Taste for salt and pepper, and adjust as needed.

Photograph by Nicole Hylton Richards.

5. Remove and reserve the corn pieces. Remove and discard the corn cobs and thyme sprigs.

6. Remove the pot from the heat. Using a hand blender, puree the soup until smooth, then add the corn pieces back to the pot.

7. Cook for another 15 minutes over low heat.

8. Ladle portions into bowls, add pieces of corn to each. Garnish with cilantro sprigs.

Vegetable or Seafood Stock

BY CHEF IRIE

As opposed to using plain water, stocks create a flavorful base for cooking. You utilize food products that you would normally throw away—like fish bones, chicken bones, shrimp shells, and bits and pieces of vegetables—to make a delicious broth. This broth becomes the foundation for soups, stews, gravies, rice dishes, potatoes, and any other dish you want to boost flavor in.

½ yellow onion, roughly chopped

2 sprigs fresh thyme

2 ribs celery

¼ cup fresh parsley stems (not leaves)

1 teaspoon allspice berries

2 carrots, washed and chopped

2 bay leaves

For Seafood Stock

4 cups shrimp shells

1 uncooked grouper or other white fish head, cut into pieces

In a large stockpot, combine all the ingredients with 8 cups water and bring to a boil. Boil for about 30 minutes, then strain and allow to cool. Use immediately, refrigerate for up to 3 days, or freeze.

Chicken Stock

BY CHEF IRIE

2 pounds chicken bones, cooked or uncooked

½ medium yellow onion, roughly chopped

2 sprigs fresh thyme

2 ribs celery

¼ cup fresh parsley stems (not leaves)

1 teaspoon allspice berries

2 carrots, washed and chopped

2 bay leaves

Method

1. If using uncooked bones, blanch the bones in hot water for 5 minutes. Discard the water.

2. In a large stockpot, combine the bones, all the remaining ingredients, and 8 cups water and bring to a boil. Boil for about 45 minutes. Strain and allow to cool. Use immediately, refrigerate for up to 3 days, or freeze.

Beef Stock

BY CHEF IRIE

3 pounds beef neck bones

1 cup olive oil

1 tablespoon kosher salt

1 tablespoon black pepper

½ medium yellow onion, roughly chopped

2 sprigs fresh thyme

2 ribs celery

¼ cup fresh parsley stems (not leaves)

1 teaspoon allspice berries

2 carrots, washed and chopped

2 bay leaves

2 tablespoons tomato paste (optional)

1. Preheat the oven to 400°F.
2. Season the neck bones with the oil, salt, and pepper. Place on a rimmed baking sheet and roast for 30 to 40 minutes.
3. In a large stockpot, combine the bones, all the remaining ingredients, and 8 cups water and bring to a boil, then reduce the heat to medium-low and simmer for 1 hour. Strain and allow to cool. Use immediately, refrigerate for up to 3 days, or freeze.

Cream of Pumpkin Soup

BY CHEF THIA

It's a Haitian tradition to drink a pumpkin soup called *soup joumou* on New Year's Day, which is when we celebrate our independence. We believe that this soup will bring happiness and good luck in the New Year.

My version is creamy and smooth. Serve this soup with a crusty bread or a French baguette.

Serves 4

2 potatoes, peeled

4 pounds calabaza pumpkin, cubed

2 tablespoons canola oil

5 tablespoons unsalted butter

1 onion, diced

2 scallions, roughly chopped

¼ cup diced garlic

¼ cup diced red bell pepper

1 tablespoon chopped fresh flat-leaf parsley

Leaves from 1 sprig fresh thyme

2½ cups vegetable stock

1½ tablespoons salt

½ teaspoon black pepper

⅔ cup heavy cream

2 fresh basil leaves, finely chopped

Red pepper flakes

1. Boil the potatoes and calabaza separately in water until fork tender, then drain. When cool enough to handle, peel the squash pieces.

2. Set a large stock pot over medium heat, then add the oil and butter. When hot, add the onion, scallions, garlic, bell pepper, and parsley and sauté until onion is translucent, about 2 minutes. Add the thyme and let the flavor incorporate for another 2 minutes.

3. Cut the potatoes into large chunks and add to the pot along with the squash, then mix everything together.

4. Add the stock, salt, and pepper and bring to a boil. Remove from the heat and allow to cool.

5. Add the cream to the pot. Spoon batches of the pumpkin and potato with the liquid into a blender, then blend and strain into another large pot.

6. Once the entire mixture has been blended and strained, reheat over medium heat and reduce for 10 minutes to thicken.

7. Ladle into bowls and garnish with basil and red pepper flakes.

Chef Thia's tip: Don't try to peel the pumpkin raw! Boil it first, cool, then peel when the skin is soft.

Black Bean Soup

BY CHEF THIA

Black bean soup is made all over the Caribbean, and everyone has a different way of doing it. Mine is like I'm cooking for myself, home-style with a little bit of bacon. The labels "soup" and "sauce" are almost interchangeable in the Haitian version of this dish. It is thick, and usually served with rice and any type of meat that's not bathed in a different sauce.

Serves 4

2 tablespoons unsalted butter, plus more for serving

½ cup bacon cut crosswise into ¼-inch strips

2 tablespoons minced red bell pepper

½ cup finely diced onion

3 fresh flat-leaf parsley sprigs

2 (30-ounce) cans organic black beans

3 tablespoons Chef Thia's Spice (page 66)

½ teaspoon salt

½ teaspoon black pepper

¼ teaspoon ground cumin

1. Melt the butter in a medium pot over high heat. Add the bacon and render until brown, 5 to 8 minutes.

2. Add the bell pepper and onion and stir until the bell pepper starts to change color and the onion is translucent, about 3 minutes.

3. Add the parsley and stir for another minute, then reduce the heat to low. Simmer for about 5 minutes to meld the flavors into the butter.

4. When the parsley has become discolored, remove it with tongs or a fork. Add one can of the beans to the pot.

5. Blend Chef Thia's Spice and the other can of black beans until smooth. Strain through a fine strainer into the pot, pressing with a large spoon or spatula, until all the puree has been pushed through. Discard the solids in the strainer.

6. Stir in the salt, pepper, and cumin, tasting and adjusting as necessary. Increase the heat to medium-low and simmer for 10 to 15 minutes, until warmed through.

7. Spoon into bowls, garnishing each with a pat of butter, to serve.

Chef Thia's tip: **Serve with a wedge of lime to brighten the flavor.**

Guava Mint Sauce

BY CHEF IRIE

Lamb dishes are typically served with some type of mint sauce, so to create a Caribbean profile, I added some guava paste. I recommend using the prepared guava paste rather than trying to make a guava reduction from scratch. Bring the paste to room temperature—it will dissolve more quickly.

Pair this sauce with any hearty protein like steak, pork, or chicken. It can also be used as a glaze or dipping sauce on the side.

2 cups orange juice

¾ cup guava paste

⅓ cup diced onion

2 tablespoons minced garlic

½ cup fresh mint leaves, chopped

½ teaspoon salt

½ teaspoon black pepper

1. Combine all of the ingredients in a medium saucepan over medium-high heat and bring to a boil, stirring occasionally.
2. Reduce the heat to medium and simmer for 20 minutes, until the sauce has reduced and thickened. Serve.

Chadon Beni Sauce

BY CHEF IRIE

Chadon beni sauce is a Trinidadian condiment that prominently features the herb culantro or *chadon beni* (pronounced "shadow benny"), a robust herb found in many Caribbean countries. The sauce is tangy and slightly spicy. I add Scotch bonnet to my version for added flavor and some heat.

Pair *chadon beni* sauce with any protein as a garnish or as a marinade. You can substitute basil or parsley if you can't find culantro.

6 scallions

1½ cup culantro, roughly chopped

10 small garlic cloves

2 teaspoons brown sugar

1 teaspoon kosher salt

1 teaspoon black pepper

1 Scotch bonnet pepper, whole with stem removed

¼ cup fresh lime juice

3 tablespoons canola oil

Put all of the ingredients except the oil in a food processor and blend. While the sauce is blending, slowly add the oil through the feed tube and continue to process until smooth.

Sauce Chien

BY CHEF IRIE

Sauce chien, literally translated from French as "dog sauce," is so named because of its sharp bite from the heat of the Scotch bonnet peppers. This recipe is unusual because of its heat level, and the fact that it is made with hot water to smooth the sauce as it blends.

It is meant to be paired with shellfish like scallops, clams, mussels, or shrimp.

½ cup roughly chopped white onion

1 cup fresh flat-leaf parsley leaves

5 cloves garlic, roughly chopped

1 tablespoon dried oregano

1 Scotch bonnet pepper, whole with stem removed

½ bouillon cube

2 scallions

1 tablespoon dry adobo seasoning

¼ cup fresh marjoram leaves

2 tablespoons fresh lime juice

¼ cup canola oil

1 tablespoon Dijon mustard

¾ cup hot water

1. Put all of the ingredients except the water in a food processor and pulse a few times until roughly combined.

2. Add the hot water and continue to pulse until the consistency is saucy, but still a bit coarse. Allow the sauce to sit for up to 1 hour for maximum flavor.

Mango Chutney

BY CHEF IRIE

Chutney is a type of savory condiment from Indian and Middle Eastern cultures, originally intended as a way to preserve ripe or unripe fruit. In this case, I chose to make a mango chutney, but you can use tamarind, golden apples, or a number of other fruit or even vegetables for a variety of sweet, savory, or tangy results. It can be eaten warm or cold with seafood, chicken, or pork.

1 semi-ripe mango, diced (or about 2 cups frozen mango chunks)

2 teaspoons chopped fresh ginger

1 teaspoon grated nutmeg

1 teaspoon ground cinnamon

1 teaspoon ground ginger

¼ teaspoon salt

4 tablespoons brown sugar

1 cup orange juice

1 tablespoon unsalted butter

1 tablespoon fresh lime juice

½ Scotch bonnet pepper, seeded and julienned

2 pods star anise

1. Combine all ingredients in a heavy, medium-size pot. Bring to a boil, then reduce the heat and simmer for about 30 minutes, until the mango chunks are soft and translucent and the sauce has thickened. Serve warm or refrigerate and serve cold. Store refrigerated in an airtight glass container for up to a month.

Tomato Rum Sauce

BY CHEF IRIE

This sauce has a slightly tart taste with some bite from the ginger, a hint of sweetness from the apples, and caramel notes in the dark rum. Pair it with any poultry or hearty fish dish. I serve this sauce with my Herb-Crusted Salmon.

2 tablespoons olive oil

½ white onion, chopped

3 cloves garlic, chopped

1 tablespoon chopped fresh ginger

1 Granny Smith or Gala apple, peeled and diced

2 tablespoons brown sugar

1 teaspoon ground cumin

1 teaspoon ground coriander

1 teaspoon paprika

2 to 3 plum tomatoes, hand squeezed

2 tablespoons tomato paste

1 teaspoon red pepper flakes

¼ cup dark Caribbean rum

1 cup chicken or vegetable stock

½ chayote squash, peeled and diced

2 teaspoons garlic powder

½ teaspoon kosher salt

¼ teaspoon black pepper

4 sprigs fresh thyme

½ cup flat-leaf parsley leaves, roughly chopped

1. In a large pot over medium heat, heat the oil, then sauté the onion, garlic, and ginger for 2 minutes, until they begin to soften.
2. Add the apple, brown sugar, cumin, coriander, and paprika and stir for about 2 minutes.
3. Add the squeezed tomato, tomato paste, and red pepper flakes and stir for another 2 minutes.
4. Add the rum, stock, chayote, garlic powder, salt, black pepper, and thyme. Stir to combine. Reduce the heat to medium-low and cook for 6 to 10 minutes, stirring periodically. Stir in the parsley, then cook for another 2 minutes. Taste and adjust the seasoning if necessary. Serve hot.

Mango Ketchup

BY CHEF IRIE

This dish was inspired by my visits to Trinidad. Ketchup is a popular condiment there, and to emphasize the versatility of fruit, I chose mango as the base for a unique twist. This sauce is less acidic than tomato ketchup and will have a varying degree of sweetness depending on the ripeness of the mangoes used. This recipe also has a little heat from the Scotch bonnet pepper.

My mango ketchup pairs nicely with Chef Irie's Trini Shark and Red Cabbage Slaw to make bake and shark. You can also serve it any time you'd serve regular ketchup.

2 ripe mangoes

2 tablespoons apple cider vinegar

2 tablespoons distilled white vinegar

½ teaspoon kosher salt

1 teaspoon ground coriander

2 tablespoons brown sugar

2 cloves garlic

1 tablespoon minced fresh ginger

½ Scotch bonnet pepper with seeds (for a spicier ketchup, use a whole pepper)

½ cup dark Caribbean rum

1. Peel the mangoes and cut the flesh from the pits. Add the mango flesh and all the remaining ingredients to a food processor or blender and puree until smooth.
2. Pour the puree into a heavy-bottomed saucepan and bring to a simmer over medium-low heat. Simmer for 1 hour, or until reduced and thickened. Allow the ketchup to cool, then transfer to an airtight container and refrigerate for up to 2 weeks.

Chef Irie's tip: Be careful not to touch your skin or eyes after touching the Scotch bonnet pepper seeds, before thoroughly washing your hands. They are extremely hot!

Chef Thia's Spice

BY CHEF THIA

Epis is a spice blend that people in Haiti use as a seasoning base for their food. Every Haitian creates their own version, and this is mine.

As a single mother who cooks almost every day, I usually don't have time to whip up lots of little components for each meal. So I make my spice in batches and put it on everything! I put it on fish with some lime; on chicken along with salt, pepper, and mustard; and on all kinds of other food. The recipe is pretty flexible. Depending on the food that I'm seasoning I might change the ingredients and amounts, so feel free to make your own adjustments to suit your family's palate too.

Makes 4 to 5 cups

1 cup canola oil

1½ cups whole garlic cloves

6 scallions, roughly chopped

1 bunch fresh curly parsley

½ bunch fresh flat-leaf parsley

10 sprigs fresh thyme

½ green bell pepper, roughly chopped

1 red bell pepper, roughly chopped

1 teaspoon whole cloves

3 chicken bouillon cubes

2 yellow onions, diced

1. Put the oil, garlic, scallions, both parsleys, and thyme in a food processor and pulse a few times to finely chop.
2. Add the bell peppers, cloves, bouillon cubes, and onion and blend until smooth. Store in an airtight glass or plastic container for up to 2 weeks in the refrigerator, or 2 months in the freezer.

Chef Thia's tip: Use as a marinade or seasoning.

Pineapple Sugarcane Glaze

BY CHEF IRIE

There's a special place in my heart for sugarcane, as I grew up on a sugar estate in Jamaica. This dish gives me a perfect opportunity to incorporate one of my favorite ingredients into a dish.

I pair the glaze with pork loin, but you can also put it on vegetables, use it to make candied carrots, or even glaze your Thanksgiving turkey with it. If you want a sweeter sauce I would suggest using very ripe pineapples.

1 cup fresh sugarcane juice

1½ cups fresh pineapple skin

¼ cup finely diced fresh pineapple

¼ cup pineapple preserves

2 to 3 cloves garlic, sliced

1 tablespoon thinly sliced fresh ginger

3 pods star anise

½ teaspoon red pepper flakes

½ teaspoon kosher salt

¼ teaspoon black pepper

1 teaspoon ground cumin

3 tablespoons fresh lime juice

2 sprigs fresh thyme

½ cup dark Caribbean rum

1 tablespoon canola oil

2 cinnamon sticks

1. Combine all the ingredients in a medium stockpot and simmer on low for 20 to 25 minutes. Remove and discard the pineapple skin, thyme stems, star anise, and cinnamon sticks, then puree the sauce in a blender.
2. Return the puree to the pot and simmer for 10 minutes. Serve warm or at room temperature.

Pineapple Salsa

BY CHEF THIA

This is a simple salsa, spicy and tart. A lot of chefs add sugar, but I don't, so the only sweetness will come from the pineapple itself.

Make sure to use a very ripe pineapple. It should smell heavenly sweet even before you peel it. Serve with burgers, grilled chicken, or fish for a summery side.

Serves 4

2 cups cubed fresh pineapple (½-inch cubes)

½ cup finely diced red onion

1½ tablespoons fresh lemon juice

¼ cup minced fresh cilantro

2 heaping tablespoons minced fresh curly parsley

¼ cup finely diced red bell pepper

½ teaspoon light brown sugar

¼ teaspoon salt

¼ teaspoon black pepper

1 tablespoon olive oil

½ teaspoon red pepper flakes

Combine all the ingredients in a medium mixing bowl and stir together. Serve.

Chimichurri Sauce

BY CHEF THIA

Chimichurri sauce is a pungent, parsley-based sauce with onion, vinegar, and spices. The acid from the red wine vinegar really brings out the flavor of meats, especially fatty grilled steaks. I use red pepper flakes for a little heat, and both red and white onions, because each brings a different flavor.

I pair this chimichurri sauce with my Churrasco Beef (page 134), but you could use it on other grilled meats too.

2½ cups red wine vinegar

1 small white onion, finely chopped

1 small red onion, finely chopped

½ medium red bell pepper, finely chopped

2 teaspoons kosher salt

½ teaspoon black pepper

2 tablespoons red pepper flakes

1 cup finely chopped fresh curly parsley

1 cup finely chopped fresh flat-leaf parsley

½ cup minced fresh cilantro

1½ cups olive oil

1. Combine the vinegar, onions, bell pepper, salt, black pepper, and red pepper flakes in a medium mixing bowl and stir well.

2. Add the parsleys, cilantro, and oil and stir to combine.

3. Serve.

4

Seafood

Seafood is an omnipresent protein in the Caribbean region. It's no surprise, when a food source like the ocean can be just steps away from many villages and cities. Fish, shellfish, mollusks (like octopus), and even river shrimp are common fare, and you'll find them incorporated into every meal of the day, from Jamaican ackee and saltfish for breakfast, to Trinidadian bake and shark for a late-night snack.

Because of the easy access and relative bounty, seafood is often cheap. On a recent Barbados trip, our team enjoyed fresh grilled mahi sandwiches for less than the cost of a frozen burger from a fast-food joint! And depending on where you are in the islands, you'll find people enjoying seafood in some very interesting ways, including the curious pleasure of seeing islanders pulling the translucent, squirmy "worm" out of a freshly caught queen conch and slurping it down right on the spot.

In some circles, the fishermen and -women who populate fishing villages are considered "unskilled labor," but that impression misunderstands the relationship these folks have with the sea. They may not have multi-ton barges from which to conduct their business, but their skill with spears and nets ensures that through hurricanes and droughts, through booming and busted world markets, their families and customers remain fed.

Interestingly, codfish, which is not native to the Caribbean, is one of the most widely consumed types of seafood in the region, stemming from its prolific use during the days of the slave trade as a preserved form of protein for the long ship rides across oceans. Find it sautéed in Antiguan or Trinidadian *buljol*, served cold in St. Lucian green fig salad or Haitian *chiquetaille* (ceviche), made into fritters in Cuba, or stewed in Puerto Rican *guisado* and in the national dish of St. Kitts and Nevis.

Please enjoy this selection of seafood recipes from the *Taste the Islands* kitchen!

Creole Shrimp

BY CHEF IRIE

This dish has Caribbean and African roots. The sauce is spicy, sweet, and acidic from the tomatoes. When served with Camarofongo (Smashed Plantains), which absorbs the creole sauce well, this dish becomes a complete meal with plenty of protein, starch, and vegetables. If you want something extra on the side, a good choice would be my Kale Salad (page 19) or Pineapple Pepper Slaw (page 20).

Serves 3 to 4

15 medium raw shrimp, peeled and deveined

1 tablespoon canola oil

1 teaspoon salt

1 teaspoon black pepper

1 teaspoon paprika

½ teaspoon red pepper flakes

For the Creole Sauce

2 tablespoons canola oil

1 tablespoon minced fresh garlic

2 tablespoons minced fresh ginger

½ cup diced green bell pepper

⅓ cup diced red bell pepper

¼ cup diced red onion

¼ cup diced white onion

½ cup finely diced celery

2 teaspoons kosher salt

1 teaspoon black pepper

½ teaspoons paprika

1 tablespoon garlic powder

1 teaspoon red pepper flakes

1 tablespoon ground cumin

1 cup chopped Roma tomatoes

1½ cups tomato sauce

2 tablespoons Worcestershire sauce

2 cups chicken stock

1 tablespoon dried oregano

4 sprigs fresh thyme

3 tablespoons chopped fresh flat-leaf parsley leaves

1. Season the shrimp with the oil, salt, black pepper, paprika, and red pepper flakes and toss to evenly coat. Set aside in the refrigerator for at least 30 minutes.
2. Make the creole sauce: In a large pan over medium heat, heat the oil. Add the fresh garlic and ginger and sauté for 1 minute.

3. Add the bell peppers, onions, and celery and cook, stirring occasionally, until the onions are translucent, 2 to 3 minutes.

4. Add the salt, black pepper, paprika, garlic powder, red pepper flakes, and cumin and stir. Cook for 1 to 2 minutes.

5. Add the tomatoes, tomato sauce, Worcestershire sauce, and stock, then stir to combine. Reduce the heat to medium-low and cook for 10 to 15 minutes, stirring occasionally, until the sauce thickens slightly.

6. Stir in the oregano and thyme, and continue to cook until the sauce has thickened.

7. Add the shrimp and parsley and stir. Continue to cook for 2 to 3 minutes, until the shrimp are pink and opaque.

8. Serve hot over a bed of Camarofongo (Smashed Plantains) (page 146).

Honey Pineapple Shrimp

BY CHEF THIA

This dish has a sweet-and-sour flavor, and the honey is pretty subtle. I like to serve it with sautéed or grilled vegetables.

Serves 2

1 teaspoon minced garlic

2 tablespoons pineapple juice

½ cup diced fresh pineapple

1 tablespoon soy sauce

1 teaspoon brown sugar

1 tablespoon finely diced red bell pepper

1 tablespoon finely diced green bell pepper

¼ teaspoon black pepper

3 tablespoons raw honey

Canola oil

1 cup precooked large shrimp, peeled and deveined

1 tablespoon finely chopped fresh curly parsley

1. In a medium bowl, combine the garlic, pineapple juice, pineapple, soy sauce, brown sugar, bell peppers, black pepper, and honey.
2. Brush a nonstick sauté pan with oil.
3. Over medium heat, sauté the shrimp for 2½ minutes on each side. Remove the shrimp when they're a bit more firm and pink.
4. Spoon the solid components of the pineapple mixture into the same pan and sauté until caramelized, about 3 minutes, stirring gently. Remove the pineapple mixture from the pan and set aside.
5. Add the liquids remaining in the bowl to deglaze the pan.
6. Reduce for about 5 minutes, until the juice has thickened into a sauce.
7. Plate the pineapple mixture, top with shrimp, then pour the sauce over the dish.
8. Garnish with the parsley and serve.

Spicy Cajun Shrimp Salad

BY CHEF THIA

This is not your typical salad. In this recipe I pan-sear spicy, creole-seasoned shrimp and serve them over a salad with bell peppers, peas, cranberries, and almonds dressed in a sweet-and-spicy pineapple dressing.

The shrimp is delicious enough to enjoy on its own over jasmine rice, if you're in a hurry. To avoid clumps of spice on your shrimp, whisk the marinade first, before adding the shrimp.

Serves 2

For the Shrimp

5 to 8 large precooked shrimp, peeled

2 teaspoons Cajun seasoning

¼ teaspoon black pepper

¼ teaspoon salt

Juice of 1 lemon

2 tablespoons olive oil

For the Pineapple Dressing

2 tablespoons pineapple preserves

¼ teaspoon ground coriander

½ teaspoon salt

¼ teaspoon black pepper

½ heaping teaspoon Cajun seasoning

¼ cup red wine vinegar

⅛ teaspoon olive oil

For the Salad

½ cup sliced raw almonds

1 tablespoon olive oil

½ cup julienned yellow bell pepper

½ cup julienned orange bell pepper

½ cup julienned red bell pepper

¼ cup cooked green peas, at room temperature

1 white onion, halved and thinly sliced

2 cups spring mix salad greens

1 small cucumber, spiral-cut thin

¼ cup dried cranberries

1. Make the shrimp: Butterfly the shrimp by cutting down the middle on the back of the shrimp, without slicing all the way through.

2. In a small bowl, combine the Cajun seasoning, pepper, salt, lemon juice, and 1 tablespoon of the oil.

3. Pour the mixture onto the shrimp and mix by hand until shrimp are completely coated. Put in the refrigerator to marinate for at least 30 minutes.

4. Pan-sear shrimp in the remaining 1 tablespoon oil over medium heat for 3 to 4 minutes to warm it through.

5. Make the pineapple dressing: In a small bowl, combine the pineapple preserves, coriander, salt, pepper, Cajun seasoning, vinegar, and oil and whisk until emulsified.

6. Make the salad: Sauté the almonds in the oil over medium heat until brown, about 2 minutes.

7. Toss all the remaining salad ingredients together with the pineapple dressing and plate. Top with the shrimp and almonds and serve.

Mussels Chorizo in Mango Coconut Sauce

BY CHEF IRIE

A trip to Spain gave me the inspiration to make this, and it has become one of my signature dishes. I utilize chorizo sausage and mussels, cooked in a simple way, and highlight Caribbean flavors with coconut, mango, and jalapeño pepper. This is a bold and rustic stand-alone dish. I recommend having it with a nice glass of chilled white wine.

Serves 4 to 6

1 to 2 pounds fresh mussels

3 tablespoons canola or olive oil

¼ cup chopped red onion

4 cloves garlic, sliced

¼ teaspoon chopped fresh ginger

¼ cup diced red and green bell peppers

½ small jalapeño pepper, diced

2 teaspoons cumin seeds

4 links Spanish cured chorizo, casings removed and roughly chopped

2 sprigs fresh thyme

1 cup Sauvignon Blanc wine

1 cup diced mango

½ cup cherry tomatoes

1 cup coconut milk

¼ teaspoon lemon zest

2 tablespoons unsalted butter

1 teaspoon black pepper

¼ cup chopped fresh cilantro

Rustic bread or baguette, sliced and toasted

1. Prepare the mussels by washing them and removing any visible beards (threadlike fibers emerging from the shell). To check for dead mussels, which should be discarded, tap them on the edge of a bowl. If they close, they are good. If they stay open, they're dead. Throw them out.

2. Add oil to a sauté pan over medium heat. Add the onion, garlic, and ginger and sauté for 1 minute, then add the peppers and cumin. Sauté for 2 minutes, then add the chorizo and thyme and sauté for another 2 minutes.

3. Add the wine, stir, and add the mango, tomatoes, and mussels. Cover the pan and reduce the heat. Cook until all the mussels have opened, 3 to 5 minutes, then add the coconut milk and lemon zest. Cover again for another 2 to 3 minutes, then add the butter, black pepper, and cilantro. Stir and remove from the heat.

4. Transfer to a bowl, place toasted bread slices attractively on top, and serve.

Seared Scallops with Sauce Chien

BY CHEF IRIE

Scallops are amazing when they are cooked correctly. There should be a crunchy crust on both sides of the scallop, and the inside should be soft and a little sweet. The general rule of seafood preparations is never to overcook, because the seafood will become hard or rubbery, and scallops certainly do become rubbery when overcooked. You want to cook them no more than 2 minutes on each side, depending on the size of the scallop. They are also great for grilling.

Serve with Sauce Chien and pair with my Celery Salad (page 16), a risotto, anything that is mashed, a quinoa salad, or a green salad.

Serves 3 to 4

10 to 12 large bay scallops

1½ teaspoons garlic powder

1 teaspoon black pepper

½ teaspoon kosher salt

2 teaspoons paprika

1½ teaspoons ground cumin

1 teaspoon red pepper flakes

4 tablespoons canola oil

Sauce Chien (page 58)

1. Gently peel off and discard the "foot" or appendage of each scallop. Put the scallops, garlic powder, black pepper, salt, paprika, cumin, red pepper flakes, and 1 tablespoon of the oil in a large bowl and toss to coat. Put a few handfuls of ice in a larger bowl, and nest the bowl of scallops within it to maintain freshness. Allow the scallops to rest.

2. Heat the remaining 3 tablespoons of oil in a frying pan over high heat. When the oil is hot, add the scallops and sear until a golden brown crust begins to form, 2 to 3 minutes per side. Scallops are done when they are easily removed from the pan, and offer slight resistance when their centers are poked with your finger.

3. Serve with Sauce Chien.

Snapper Ceviche

BY CHEF IRIE

Ceviches are seafood salads cooked in acidic juices rather than heat, and are very common in Latin countries. They offer a mélange of textures and flavors: the tanginess of the citrus that is used to "cook" the seafood, a little sweetness from tropical fruit, and of course the crunch of ingredients like corn and peppers. I like a little kick in my ceviche, but many people choose not to include any hot peppers.

Serves 4

1 pound fresh snapper fillet, skins removed

¾ cup fresh lime juice

1 cup orange juice

½ teaspoon red pepper flakes

4 to 5 cherry tomatoes, sliced

¼ cup diced ripe but firm mangoes

¼ cup diced red and green bell peppers

¼ cup julienned red onion

¼ teaspoon chopped fresh ginger

¼ teaspoon diced jalapeño pepper

1 teaspoon fresh thyme leaves

1 teaspoon salt

1 teaspoon black pepper

¼ cup chopped fresh cilantro

Fresh cilantro sprigs and Plantain Chips (page 2)

1. Cut the snapper into ½-inch cubes, put in a bowl, and add one-quarter of the lime and orange juices. Place that bowl into another with ice and set aside for 10 minutes.

2. Drain the snapper and place in a clean medium bowl.

3. Add the red pepper flakes, tomatoes, mangoes, bell peppers, onion, ginger, and jalapeño.

4. Add the remaining lime and orange juices, the thyme, salt and pepper to taste, and the chopped cilantro.

5. Mix together all ingredients and spoon into martini glasses.

6. Place in the refrigerator until ready to serve.

7. Garnish with cilantro sprigs and plantain chips and serve.

Chef Irie's tip: Use snapper, mahi, tuna, or any other firm white fish, or shellfish including shrimp or scallops. You can use lemon, lime, orange, or grapefruit juice as your acid. Use fish or seafood within 2 days of purchase for maximum freshness.

Photograph by Nicole Hylton Richards.

Red Snapper Fillet

BY CHEF THIA

I like simplicity. This red snapper fillet is simple and delicious, with crispy skin, and light citrus and garlic flavors. I serve this dish with my Roasted Potato Slices (page 166).

Make sure you sauté the fillet with the skin side down first, so it gets nice and crispy.

Serves 2

2 teaspoons garlic paste

1 tablespoon olive oil

Juice of 1 lemon

¼ teaspoon salt

⅛ teaspoon black pepper

12 ounces snapper fillet, skin on

1. Mix together the garlic paste, oil, lemon juice, salt, and pepper to create a marinade. Rub over the fillet and let marinate for 10 to 20 minutes.
2. Heat a heavy, nonstick pan over high heat, and sear the fillet skin side down until it is dark brown, about 4 minutes. Flip and sear for about 3 minutes, or until the flesh turns white in the center. Serve.

Snapper en Papillote

BY CHEF IRIE

En papillote is a method of cooking in which food is wrapped in a paper parcel and baked in the oven. It's easy to do, and the result is a complete meal. Inside this papillote, snapper steams with butter, seasonings, and vegetables; the steam is the secret, making everything moist and tasty. The vegetables should still have a slight crunchiness. Coconut milk can be added for a little extra sweetness and creaminess.

This is a stand-alone meal that you could serve with a small salad and a glass of rum or wine. You can use this method with any fish, seafood, cut of meat, or vegetables, but I wanted to showcase the snapper fish. You'll need sheets of parchment paper for this recipe.

Serves 2

2 large snapper fillets

3 to 4 tablespoons olive oil

1 tablespoon salt

1 tablespoon black pepper

1 tablespoon garlic powder

1 tablespoon ground coriander

¼ cup julienned red onion

¼ cup julienned red bell pepper

¼ cup julienned carrot

½ cup cherry tomatoes, halved

1 tablespoon fresh thyme leaves, no stems

1 teaspoon julienned Scotch bonnet pepper

1 tablespoon julienned jalapeño pepper

1 tablespoon thinly sliced garlic

1 teaspoon finely diced fresh ginger

¼ cup coconut milk

Zest of 1 lemon

2 tablespoons cold unsalted butter

¼ cup fresh flat-leaf parsley or cilantro leaves, roughly chopped

1. Preheat the oven to 375°F.

2. Rub the fillets with the oil and season with salt, black pepper, garlic powder, and coriander.

3. Off center, divided between two sheets of parchment paper, place the

onion, bell pepper, carrot, and tomatoes, then top with thyme leaves, Scotch bonnet, jalapeño, fresh garlic, and ginger.

4. Place the fillets on top of the vegetables. Over each fillet, drizzle coconut milk, sprinkle lemon zest, add a tablespoon of butter, and scatter the cilantro leaves.

5. Fold the parchment paper in half to form a pouch over the fish, then crimp one corner of the sheet and roll all the way around the edges to tightly seal the pouch.

6. Bake for 20 to 30 minutes. The pouch will puff up as the fish roasts. To serve, cut a hole in the top of the pouch, and tear away the paper to release the steam.

Chef Irie's tip: If the flavor of the fish needs to be "brightened," add lemon juice for acidity.

Roasted Red Snapper

BY CHEF IRIE

We eat a lot of red snapper in the Caribbean, either fried, steamed, or roasted. Snapper is firm enough to hold up well when cooked, its mild taste takes on the flavors of what it's cooked with. In Jamaica, when a snapper is roasted, it is traditionally stuffed with whole, thick water crackers, which become a tasty side once softened and flavored by the roasting process. Try pairing snapper with Mashed Yellow Yam (page 150), which also absorbs the serving sauce. Other good options are roasted potatoes or sweet potatoes, roasted vegetables, or rice.

When you pick out your fish, make sure it smells fresh. The market should smell like the ocean; if the market smells like ammonia, I would not recommend buying your fish there. Also, ask the fishmonger to touch the fish to make sure the flesh is firm, not spongy, and check that the eyes are clear, not cloudy.

Serves 3

- 3 whole red snapper (up to 2 pounds each)
- 3 tablespoons garlic powder
- 3 tablespoons onion powder
- 2 tablespoons black pepper
- 2 tablespoons kosher salt
- 6 whole pods okra
- 3 sprigs fresh thyme
- ½ cup peeled and julienned chayote
- ½ cup julienned carrot
- ½ cup sliced yellow onion
- ½ cup fresh flat-leaf parsley leaves
- 1 tablespoon julienned fresh ginger
- 2 Scotch bonnet peppers, julienned
- 3 water crackers
- 3 tablespoons unsalted butter

1. Rinse each snapper and pat dry. Make 2 or 3 shallow diagonal slits on both sides of each fish, being careful not to cut all the way through to the cavity.
2. In a small bowl, make a seasoning blend with the garlic powder, onion powder, black pepper, and salt. Sprinkle the outsides of the fish with the blend, rubbing into the skin and slits.
3. Cut the ends off the okra and cut in half lengthwise. Stuff the cavity of each fish with okra halves, a sprig of thyme, and one-third of the chayote, carrot, onion, parsley, ginger, and Scotch bonnet. Lay one whole water

cracker in the cavity of each fish, on top of the vegetables. Slather a tablespoon of butter on top of each fish.

4. Wrap each fish in foil, creating a tight packet.

5. Preheat a grill to medium-high heat. When the grill is hot, lay out the fish packets on the grate and grill each side for 15 minutes. If using a hooded grill, cover and grill for 30 minutes without flipping, as the heat will circulate around the pouch. Allow the fish to rest for 2 to 3 minutes after removing them from the grill before serving.

Escoveitch Fish

BY CHEF IRIE

This Mediterranean dish originated in Spain and Portugal. In the Caribbean, the fish is coated in flour and fried until crispy, then pickled in a tangy, spicy sauce. Pair this dish with a simple Jamaican hard dough bread, fried *bammy*, fried dumplings, or cornmeal festival.

Make sure that the fish is fried in a good amount of oil to get a nice crispiness on the outside, and don't overcook the fish or it will be dry.

Serves 4

For the Seasoning Blend

2 teaspoons kosher salt

2 teaspoons ground cumin

2 teaspoons ground coriander

1 tablespoon dried marjoram

1 tablespoon fresh thyme leaves

1 teaspoon red pepper flakes

For the Fish

1 cup all-purpose flour

3 pounds snapper, grouper, or any firm white fish, filleted and cut into 2-inch slices

2 cups olive oil

¼ white onion, julienned

2 large green bell peppers, sliced

¼ cup peeled and julienned chayote

4 cloves garlic, sliced

2 Scotch bonnet peppers, julienned

¼ cup julienned carrot

1 tablespoon julienned fresh ginger

4 sprigs fresh thyme

½ cup olive oil

½ cup apple cider vinegar

1. Make the seasoning blend: Combine all the ingredients together.
2. Mix 1 tablespoon of the seasoning blend into the flour, and season the fish generously with the remaining seasoning blend. Dredge the fish slices in the seasoned flour.
3. Heat 1½ cups of the oil in a frying pan over medium-high heat. Fry the fish slices until they are golden, then place on paper towels to drain, leaving the oil in the pan.

4. Sauté the onion, bell peppers, chayote, garlic, Scotch bonnets, carrot, ginger, and thyme in the same oil.

5. Put the fish in a glass or ceramic bowl (do not use stainless steel). Add the sautéed vegetable mixture.

6. Add the remaining ½ cup oil and the vinegar to cover all of the ingredients. Cover the bowl and refrigerate overnight.

7. Remove from fridge and allow to come to room temperature before serving.

Chef Irie's Trini Shark

BY CHEF IRIE

This is a dish straight out of Trinidad, where they traditionally use shark meat in the recipe. We're using corvina instead. The name of the finished sandwich is bake and shark—*not* shark and bake—because it's really all about the bake. The "shark" is the easy part. Here we go!

Serves 2 to 4

1 tablespoon paprika

1 teaspoon salt

1 teaspoon black pepper

2 to 4 corvina fish fillets, or substitute grouper, mahi, or whiting

Canola oil for frying

1 cup all-purpose flour

1. Combine the paprika, salt, and pepper in a small bowl. Sprinkle the paprika mixture onto the fish, and allow to sit for 10 to 15 minutes.
2. Heat at least 2 inches of oil to 375°F in frying pan or deep-fryer over medium-high heat.
3. Put the flour in a small dish. Dip each side of the seasoned fish into the flour to coat.
4. Put the fish in the hot oil and fry each side for 5 to 6 minutes, until the fish floats to the surface of the oil.
5. Remove the fish and place on paper towels to drain.
6. Slice the Trinidadian Bakes (page 156), and assemble warm corvina with Red Cabbage Slaw (page 23) and Mango Ketchup (page 65) for a delicious bake and "shark" sandwich.

Ackee and Saltfish

BY CHEF IRIE

This is my take on ackee and saltfish, the national dish of Jamaica. Ackee is a fruit that has a mild flavor and a soft texture when cooked. If the ackee is over-cooked it will get mushy and start to fall apart, so you want to watch it closely if cooking from scratch, and only warm it through if cooking from the can.

The saltfish adds a salty taste to the dish. Make sure not to boil out too much of the salt, or the dish will taste bland. I add white wine for extra tang and to enhance the flavors of the other ingredients.

Serves 4

2 pounds salted codfish or bacalao in bite-size pieces

3 tablespoons canola oil

⅓ cup julienned red onion

1 tablespoon roughly chopped garlic

¼ teaspoon salt

1 Scotch bonnet pepper, finely minced

1 teaspoon black pepper

1 tablespoon chopped fresh thyme

½ cup diced fresh tomatoes

¼ cup white wine (optional)

2 (19-ounce) cans ackee, drained

1. Soak the codfish in a large bowl of water overnight, drain, then cover in fresh water and boil for about 10 minutes to reduce the salt content.

2. Drain the codfish, then break it up into small pieces and remove all bones.

3. Heat the oil in a large frying pan over medium heat. Add the onion, garlic, salt, Scotch bonnet, and half of the black pepper and sauté, stirring occasionally, until the onion begins to turn translucent.

4. Add the thyme and tomato and stir. Increase the heat to medium-high and continue to cook, stirring occasionally, for 2 to 3 minutes.

5. Add the codfish and wine and stir. Gently fold in the ackee to avoid breaking it. Continue to cook for 4 to 5 minutes, stirring very gently, until everything is heated through. Sprinkle the remaining black pepper over the top and serve.

Codfish Creole

BY CHEF THIA

In this codfish dish, I use lots of garlic and lime so that it almost tastes like ceviche, except I sauté it. Serve this dish by itself, with fried plantains, or make sliders with soft potato bread.

Serves 2

1½ pounds salted codfish in bite-size pieces

1 cup canola oil

1 cup cherry tomatoes, halved

2 teaspoons chopped garlic

¾ cup sliced yellow onion

3 tablespoons fresh lime juice

1 teaspoon minced, fresh flat-leaf parsley, plus a few fresh parsley leaves for garnish

2 scallions, sliced

Salt

1 teaspoon red pepper flakes

1 teaspoon Chef Thia's Spice (page 66)

1. Soak the codfish in a large bowl of water overnight, drain, then cover in fresh water and boil for about 10 minutes to reduce the salt content.

2. Drain the codfish, then break it up into small pieces and remove all bones.

3. Heat the oil in a frying pan over medium-high heat. When the oil is hot, add the tomatoes, stirring until they begin to change color, then add the garlic and sauté, stirring occasionally, for 2 to 3 minutes.

4. Add the codfish, onion, lime juice, minced parsley, and scallions and cook for 2 to 3 minutes.

5. Taste and add salt, if desired. Stir in the red pepper flakes and Chef Thia's spice.

6. Top with fresh parsley leaves and serve.

Lunch with the Bad Boys of Reggae

Lancelot Hall, Bernard "Touter" Harvey, and Chef Irie (*left to right*).

Behind the unforgettable refrain "Girl I Wanna Make You Sweat" and the song that sparked a movie and a television series, *Bad Boys*, is the reggae band called Inner Circle. Lancelot Hall, Bernard "Touter" Harvey, and brothers Roger and Ian Lewis welcomed us into their exclusive studio, then cooked and broke bread with Chef Irie for an unforgettable episode of the *Taste the Islands* television show.

Their iconic studios, Circle House and Circle Village, are located in sunny Miami. International stars like Alicia Keys, Flo Rida, and Pharrell Williams have recorded megahits

(Williams's "Happy," for example) within their walls. The backyard of the Circle Village property is decorated with elaborate murals and reggae symbols, and spots for a casual game of ludo or dominoes line the area around the pool and porch. Behind a wooden fence, the outer yard is dotted with mango, coconut, and star fruit trees, giving Chef Irie the opportunity to do what he does best, incorporate interesting flavors that he randomly discovers into his dish of the day.

Together with band members Lancelot and Touter, Chef Irie prepared a vermouth-infused version of Jamaican saltfish and cabbage, with the surprise element of mildly sweet, freshly picked star fruit. He then sat with the entire band to eat, laugh, and chat about their culinary memories.

They shared stories of tours before their breakout success when, with limited funds and seven men to feed, they would split a single order of Asian moo goo gai pan with extra plates . . . and lots of extra rice! In a particularly rousing exchange, they warned that no one should be casual about the start of dinnertime at Circle House. Roger said, "Come late . . ." and in unison the rest of the band chimed in, "*Lose weight!*"

The band also talked about the clean-eating principles of the Rastafarian faith, and how funny it was that the expensive, non-GMO, pesticide-free food that Americans call "organic" was simply called "food" in Jamaica when they were growing up. They recalled gathering eggs, drinking fresh milk, and living a very simple life back in the islands before finding fame as the Bad Boys of Reggae. The band is still all about their roots. ☀

Above: Lancelot Hall and Chef Irie.
Below: Lancelot Hall, Bernard "Touter" Harvey, and Chef Irie (*background, left to right*); Calibe Thompson, Lukkee Chong, Brittany Murphy, and Adam Heim (*foreground, left to right*).

Codfish and Cabbage

BY CHEF IRIE

This is my version of codfish and cabbage, traditionally a simple, budget-friendly Jamaican dish. It's a wonderful dish by itself, or you can pair it with Coucou, steamed white rice, Mashed Yellow Yam, boiled yellow yam, or fried dumplings.

Be careful not to overcook the cabbage. It should still have a little firmness.

Serves 4 to 6

1½ pounds fresh codfish

4 tablespoons olive oil

3 teaspoons Jamaican curry powder

2 teaspoons dried oregano

1 teaspoon black pepper

2 teaspoons salt

2 teaspoons ground cumin

2 teaspoons paprika

¼ cup sliced onion

3 cups shredded green cabbage

3 cups shredded red cabbage

1 tablespoon fresh thyme leaves

½ cup chopped scallions

1 Scotch bonnet pepper, seeds removed and minced

¼ cup dry white wine or vermouth

1 cup diced fresh tomatoes

3 cloves garlic, thinly sliced

1 serrano pepper, sliced

Juice of 1 lime

Star fruit (optional)

1. In a large bowl, drizzle 2 tablespoons of the oil over fresh codfish. Sprinkle the fish with curry powder, oregano, black pepper, salt, cumin, and paprika. Toss to coat.
2. Heat the remaining oil in a sauté pan over medium heat. Add the onion, cabbages, and thyme to the pan and stir together.
3. Add the scallions, Scotch bonnet, and vermouth to the pan.
4. In a separate frying pan, heat the remaining 2 tablespoons oil and add the seasoned codfish, making sure not to overcrowd the pan. Fry the fish evenly on both sides, 2 to 4 minutes per side.
5. Add the tomatoes, garlic, serrano, and lime juice to the fish, and cook for 5 to 7 minutes, until the ingredients are melded together.
6. Plate the cabbage mixture, then place the fish on the bed of cabbage and garnish with star fruit slices if using. Serve and enjoy!

Citrus Tarragon Salmon

BY CHEF THIA

This salmon is bathed in subtle herb flavors, with fresh tarragon and basil, garlic, orange juice, and chunks of fresh navel orange. Serve with roasted corn on the cob.

Serves 2

Juice of 1 lemon

⅔ cup orange juice

½ teaspoon salt

¼ teaspoon black pepper

6 large fresh basil leaves, finely chopped

6 sprigs fresh tarragon

1½ teaspoons garlic paste

2 tablespoons olive oil

10 to 12 ounces salmon fillet, skin on

1 navel orange, segmented with membranes removed

1. In a medium bowl, combine the orange and lemon juices, salt, pepper, basil, tarragon, garlic paste, and oil. Add the salmon and gently massage with the mixture. Marinate for 15 minutes.

2. Preheat the oven to 350°F.

3. In a hot frying pan, add the salmon, skin side up, along with the marinade. Cook for about 4 minutes, then flip the salmon. Add the orange segments and cook for another 2 minutes.

4. Transfer to oven to finish for about 20 minutes, then serve.

Herb-Crusted Salmon

BY CHEF IRIE

Herbs are always a great way to elevate flavor. Instead of crusting the salmon with bread crumbs or crushed plantains, herbs can be used. I would pair this dish with my Green Papaya Mango Slaw, or mashed chayote, mashed sweet boniato, curried cauliflower puree, or even lay it over mushroom risotto.

Serves 2

10 ounces salmon fillet, in two portions

3 tablespoons plus ¼ cup olive oil

2 teaspoons garlic powder

½ teaspoon paprika

2 tablespoons ground cumin

2 tablespoons ground coriander

1 tablespoon dried marjoram

1 tablespoon dried thyme leaves

1 teaspoon red pepper flakes

2 teaspoons kosher salt

2 cups Chef Irie's Tomato Rum Sauce (page 62)

1. Put the salmon in a bowl and season with the 3 tablespoons oil, the garlic powder, paprika, cumin, coriander, marjoram, thyme, red pepper flakes and salt. Cover with plastic and place in the refrigerator to chill.

2. In a large sauté pan over medium heat, heat the remaining ¼ cup oil. When hot, sear the salmon, skin side down, for 2 to 3 minutes, until golden brown. Remove the salmon from the pan and place on paper towels.

3. Add the Tomato Rum Sauce to the pan and heat. Return the salmon to the pan, seared side up, and cook uncovered for another 5 minutes. Remove to plates and serve.

5

Poultry and Meat

The types of protein that Caribbean people eat are largely a result of the ethnic ancestry and religious leanings of the regions they occupy. Although the Caribbean is predominantly populated by Africans, there are Asian, Middle Eastern, East Indian, and of course European influences that permeate the various island cultures and food.

On the islands with a strong European influence, the majority of people consume common proteins like chicken, pork, and beef, albeit prepared with island spices like hot peppers, pimento, thyme, culantro, and cilantro. Islands with a heavy African or Middle Eastern influence enjoy lots of goat meat. In the Latin islands you'll find traditional Spanish dishes like picadillo and chorizo—spiced beef and pork—incorporated into the food culture. In Haiti, you'll find turkey consumed, and lamb in Trinidad—meats less likely to be found elsewhere in the region. In Trinidad and other islands of the Lesser Antilles, some people enjoy what is called "wild meat," including iguana, agouti (a large rodent), armadillo, and deer.

Throughout all the islands, as foundations of their way of spiritual living, faith groups like Rastafarians and Seventh-Day Adventists forgo pork and beef as well as shellfish, which they consider "unclean." In Trinidad, a largely East Indian and Middle Eastern population with Hindu and Muslim orientations, beef and pork are less widely accepted, and vegetarian fare is common; meats here are often curried when they are prepared.

When it comes to cooking methods, stewing is enjoyed across the region in a seemingly endless variety of dishes, like Dutch Caribbean *carni stoba* (beef stew), Jamaican stewed peas made with pigs' tails, and Haitian *poulet creole* (stewed chicken). Grilling is a go-to method for foods such as jerk from Jamaica and Latin Caribbean *asadas*. Frying, baking, roasting, and other internationally common methods are used in all the islands. You'll also find one-pot rice and meat dishes like Latin arroz con pollo (rice with chicken) and Trinidadian *pelau*.

In this chapter, enjoy some of the traditional poultry and meat recipes our chefs have adapted.

Facing page: Photograph by Nicole Hylton Richards.

Chicken Pelau

BY CHEF IRIE

Pelau is a one-pot chicken dish from Trinidad. It stands by itself because it has plenty of starch, vegetables, protein, and a whole lot of flavor.

The trick to a great *pelau* is seasoning the chicken well and using enough browning to give the entire pot of food nice, rich color and flavor. The rice and pigeon peas will absorb the flavors of the other ingredients and the broth. Just be careful, you never want to overcook your rice.

Serves 3 or 4

For the Seasoning Blend

2 tablespoons ground ginger

2 tablespoons ground cumin

2 teaspoons paprika

1 tablespoon black pepper

2 tablespoons kosher salt

For the Pelau

3 pounds chicken leg quarters, cut into 4-inch pieces

¼ cup plus 2 tablespoons canola oil

2 tablespoons browning sauce

¼ cup brown sugar

¼ cup granulated sugar

¼ cup diced onion

1 tablespoon chopped garlic

1 cup diced fresh tomatoes

1 cup peeled and finely diced calabaza pumpkin

1 teaspoon chopped fresh ginger

1 cup canned green or brown *gandules* (pigeon peas)

3 cups parboiled rice

1 teaspoon red pepper flakes

5 cups chicken or vegetable stock

2 teaspoons salt

3 sprigs fresh thyme

2 scallions

¼ cup fresh cilantro leaves

1. Make the seasoning blend: Mix together all the ingredients.

2. Make the *pelau*: Put the chicken in a large bowl and season generously with the spice mixture and the ¼ cup oil. Add the browning sauce and mix well until the chicken pieces have taken the color of the sauce. Let stand, covered, for 1 hour or overnight in the refrigerator.

3. Remove the chicken from the fridge and let come to room temperature.

4. In a large Dutch oven or pot, combine the sugars, the remaining 2 table-spoons oil, and 2 tablespoons water. Cook over medium heat, stirring, until the sugar caramelizes and a dark golden caramel color has been reached. Add the chicken pieces to the pan. Stir around until the caramel has been absorbed and picked up by the chicken.

5. Add the onion and garlic and cook for 2 minutes. Add the tomatoes, calabaza, ginger, and pigeon peas. Stir well and cook for 2 minutes. Add the rice and stir gently until all the rice is evenly coated. Add the red pepper flakes and the stock. Add salt and seasoning to taste. Mix well.

6. Add the thyme and scallions on the top. Cover the pot and bring to a boil, then reduce the heat and simmer over medium-low heat until the liquid has been absorbed and the rice is tender. Remove from the heat and let sit, covered, for 10 to 15 minutes.

7. Use a fork to fluff the rice. Spoon into a plate or bowl, add a few cilantro leaves as garnish, and serve.

Chef Irie's tips: Replace half the stock with coconut milk for richer, slightly sweeter flavor. Calabaza pumpkin can be replaced with butternut or other fall squash. Try this dish with Chef Irie's Pineapple Pepper Slaw.

Pineapple Marmalade Chicken Brochette

BY CHEF THIA

This is a simple but interesting kebab. The chicken is a little spicy, sweet, and very moist, thanks to a marinade made with pineapple, my Chef Thia's Spice, and rum. Chunks of juicy pineapple add an acidic flavor that elevates this dish. Serve these as they are, in a wrap, or dropped on top of a salad—no dressing necessary.

Keep in mind that the longer you marinate the chicken, the better the flavor will be.

Serves 5

1 pound boneless, skinless chicken breasts, cut into 1-inch cubes

1 tablespoon Chef Thia's Spice (page 66)

½ teaspoon black pepper

1 teaspoon salt

1 tablespoon canola oil

2 tablespoons rum

½ cup pineapple preserves

1 to 2 large orange bell peppers, cut into 1-inch squares

2 red onions, cut into 1-inch squares

15 fresh pineapple chunks

2 tablespoons unsalted butter (optional)

¼ cup orange juice

Supplies

5 long wooden skewers

1. Soak wooden skewers in water for 10 minutes to avoid splintering on the grill.

2. Put the chicken in a large mixing bowl and season with Chef Thia's Spice, black pepper, salt, oil, rum, and pineapple preserves. Massage the seasoning into the chicken, then cover and refrigerate for about 10 minutes to marinate.

3. Load wooden skewers with the chicken, bell pepper, onions, and pineapple (alternating in any order you like).

4. Heat a grill pan over high heat or preheat a grill to high. Add the butter to the griddle for a smoky flavor, if desired.

5. Arrange the skewers on the grill pan so that they are not touching. Grill for 5 to 8 minutes on each side, basting the grilled sides with the orange juice, until the chicken has begun to turn white and has dark grill lines.

6. Remove from the skewers and serve plated with grilled corn and my Roasted Potato Slices (page 166).

Curried Peanut Chicken with Long Beans

BY CHEF IRIE

This dish showcases Dutch Caribbean cuisine, which is influenced by a number of other cultures, including French and Thai, as reflected by the long beans and peanut butter. This dish is nutty, salty, and slightly sweet. The chicken is firm, and the long beans should be crunchy.

Serves 4

For the Curried Peanut Chicken

2 pounds chicken thighs, deboned

1 tablespoon salt

1 teaspoon black pepper

3 tablespoons canola oil

2 tablespoons curry powder

¾ cup diced onion

1 tablespoon sliced fresh garlic

1 teaspoon red pepper flakes

1 tablespoon chopped fresh ginger

1 tablespoon garlic powder

2 teaspoons paprika

2 teaspoons ground coriander

2 teaspoons ground dried oregano

3 tablespoons fresh lime juice

4 cups hot water

1 cup peanut butter

½ cup orange juice

For the Long Beans

1 tablespoon plus 1 teaspoon salt

1 pound fresh long beans or green beans

1 tablespoon canola oil

¼ cup julienned white onion

1 teaspoon garlic powder

½ teaspoon black pepper

1 teaspoon red pepper flakes

2 tablespoons chopped fresh culantro

1 tablespoon mushroom soy sauce

Peanuts

1. Make the curried peanut chicken: Put the chicken in a large mixing bowl and season with the salt and pepper. Cover and refrigerate for up to 1 hour to marinate.

2. Heat the oil in a large frying pan over medium-high heat. When the oil is hot, add the curry powder. Remove the pan from the heat and whisk the curry and oil together until smooth.

3. Add the onion, garlic, and chicken to the pan and stir, then reduce to medium-low heat. Add the red pepper flakes, ginger, garlic powder, paprika, coriander, oregano, and lime juice. Stir and continue to cook for 2 to 3 minutes.

4. Add the hot water and the peanut butter, stir, and allow to simmer, covered, for 45 minutes to an hour.

5. Add the orange juice to the chicken and stir well. Replace the lid and continue to cook for 2 to 3 minutes, until the sauce has thickened.

6. Make the long beans: Bring a pot of water to boil, then add 1 tablespoon salt. Add the long beans to the boiling water and blanch for 90 seconds. Drain and quickly transfer the beans to a bowl of ice water to stop the cooking process. When the beans have cooled, drain them.

7. Heat the oil in a frying pan over medium heat, add the onion, and sauté for about 1 minute. Add the long beans, garlic powder, black pepper, salt, red pepper flakes, culantro, and mushroom soy sauce. Sauté for 4 to 5 minutes, then remove from the heat.

8. Sprinkle the peanuts over the beans and serve with the chicken.

Chef Irie's tip: Garnish with lime-scented peanuts for a more exotic flavor.

Tasso de Dinde (Fried Turkey Breast with Red Onions)

BY CHEF THIA

This is a classic Haitian recipe. My version is a little more upscale, with wine and tomato paste, which enhance the creole flavors. I serve this with Djon-Djon Mushroom Rice (page 162) and Tomato and Avocado Salad (page 33).

Serves 6

2 pounds lean turkey breast, chopped into 1½-inch cubes

2 teaspoons mustard

1 teaspoon red pepper flakes

1 teaspoon salt

½ teaspoon black pepper

½ cup canola oil

2 tablespoons tomato paste

½ cup white wine

½ orange or red bell pepper, diced

½ green bell pepper, diced

3 tablespoons chopped scallion

1½ cups thinly sliced red onions

½ cup turkey stock, chicken stock, or water

2 tablespoons chopped fresh parsley

1. Put the turkey in a large mixing bowl and season with the mustard, red pepper flakes, salt, and black pepper. Toss to coat. Cover and refrigerate overnight or for at least 30 minutes to marinate.

2. Heat the oil in a large frying pan over high heat. When the oil is hot, add the turkey pieces and sear for 8 to 10 minutes, or until golden brown, on each side. Remove the turkey from the pan and discard the oil.

3. Return the pan to medium heat and add the tomato paste and wine. Bring to a gentle simmer.

4. Add the bell peppers and cook until the sauce has thickened, stirring occasionally.

5. Increase the heat to medium-high and return the turkey to the pan, along with any juices it has released, the scallion, red onion, and stock. Stir, cover, and simmer for 10 to 15 minutes, until the turkey breast is soft and juicy. Sprinkle parsley over the top and remove from the heat.

6. Serve with white rice or *diri kole*.

Smoked Turkey Pumpkin Frittata

BY CHEF IRIE

The frittata is the Italian version of an omelet, made in the oven, with a variety of vegetables and proteins. My frittata incorporates Caribbean flavors like calabaza pumpkin, thyme, and jerk seasoning.

Serves 8 to 10

6 eggs, beaten

¼ cup heavy cream

1 tablespoon prepared jerk seasoning

2 tablespoons unsalted butter

½ cup diced red bell pepper

½ cup diced green bell pepper

½ cup diced red onion

2 cloves garlic, thinly sliced

1½ cups peeled and diced calabaza pumpkin

1½ cups diced smoked turkey

1 tablespoon fresh thyme leaves

1 teaspoon salt

1 teaspoon black pepper

1. Preheat the oven to 350°F.

2. Whisk the eggs with the cream and jerk seasoning in a medium bowl.

3. Add the butter to a medium sauté pan over medium heat. Add the bell peppers, onion, garlic, and calabaza and sauté for about 1 minute. Add the turkey and thyme and sauté for another 1 minute. Season with salt and black pepper. Reduce the heat to medium-low.

4. Add the whisked eggs and stir to combine the mixture in the pan. When the eggs just start to set, remove from the heat and place the pan in the oven. Bake until the frittata is set with just a slight brown on the top. Remove from the oven and let sit for about 2 minutes, until the pan is no longer piping hot.

5. Carefully, handling the pan with a dish towel, use a small knife to rim around the edge of the pan to release the frittata from the sides. Place a plate on top of the pan face side down, then invert the frittata onto the plate. It should slide out.

6. Slice the frittata into wedges and serve either warm or at room temperature.

Turkey Meatballs

BY CHEF THIA

This is my spin on my grandma's meatball recipe. The meatballs are soft, juicy, and bursting with classic Haitian flavors. I like to serve them with white rice and black bean sauce, and a creole sauce on the side.

To help the balls stay together while cooking, put them in the refrigerator for about 30 minutes before frying.

Serves 4 to 6

1 cup whole milk

½ cup Chef Thia's Spice (page 66)

1 tablespoon yellow mustard

½ teaspoon salt

¼ teaspoon black pepper

2 slices white bread, crusts removed

¼ teaspoons paprika

2½ pounds ground turkey

Canola oil for frying

1. In a large bowl, thoroughly combine all the ingredients except the oil, ensuring that the bread is totally dissolved and the seasoning is completely mixed into the turkey.
2. Roll the mixture into ½-inch balls and chill for 30 minutes.
3. In a large, heavy pot over medium-high heat, deep-fry the meatballs in canola oil for 5 to 8 minutes, until dark brown.
4. Serve with white rice or my Roasted Potato Slices (page 166).

Jamaica, Land We Love

Former Jamaican consul general to Miami Franz Hall joined Chef Irie and co-host Lisa Lee Arneaud on the set of *Taste the Islands* season 2. Chef Irie's menu for this Jamaican-themed episode included soul food options like Ackee and Saltfish, Curried Goat, and rum-spiked carrot juice along with his own uniquely created sides of Mashed Yellow Yam and Breadfruit Pumpkin Salad.

Hall shared stories of his own upbringing during that exchange, mentioning that both his parents were great cooks, and bragging about his own prowess at making "a mean rum cake." Co-host Lisa Lee Arneaud, who also has some Jamaican lineage in her family, talked about Jamaican food typically being presented in a very casual style—in a cardboard or styrofoam box, piled in tasty heaps. Chef Irie's presentation, she said, was, as usual, so much more refined.

The episode offered a glimpse into Chef Irie's own culinary roots, with an on-camera visit to the sugar plantation—Caymanas Estate—where he grew up with both his parents. There, he developed an intimate knowledge of rum, one of the byproducts of sugar, and has incorporated it into a number of his dishes, from desserts to drinks and entrées. Chef Irie shared stories about catching land crabs with his late father, and talked about the crab soup that he used to enjoy locally, as well as traditional, cassava-based bammy cakes, steamed fish, and other dishes that were available to him in his childhood.

While in Jamaica, we also filmed colorful vignettes of Kingston's Coronation Market, where vendors from across the countryside bring fresh produce to sell in town. The scene saw animated people dancing and mingling in the streets, piles of natural ingredients like peppers, yams, green bananas and plantains, and fresh fruits and vegetables.

Chef Irie, then and now, invites everyone to indulge, whenever they can, in authentic Jamaican cuisine! 🌟

Tyler Council, Adam Heim, Franz Hall, Chef Irie, Lisa Lee Arneaud, Lukkee Chong, and Brandon Mitchell (*left to right*). Photograph by Calibe Thompson.

Curried Goat

BY CHEF IRIE

Curried goat may not be the official national dish of Jamaica, but it's definitely a national treasure. I grew up loving it as a kid. It combines Indian culture, through the curry spices, with goat meat, which is eaten all over the island. There are different types of curry—some hot, some mild, and some more pungent.

This dish can be served with steamed white rice, rice and peas, Mashed Yellow Yam, boiled dumplings, or boiled bananas. Cook the curried goat until nice and tender but not mushy. It should be firm enough to chew, but not tough.

Serves 6

1½ pounds boneless goat, cut into 2-inch chunks

3 teaspoons salt

2 teaspoons black pepper

1½ teaspoons ground allspice

2 teaspoons ground coriander

1 teaspoon paprika

1½ teaspoons red pepper flakes

3 teaspoons garlic powder

3 tablespoons Jamaican curry powder, plus 1 tablespoon to burn

2 teaspoons ground cumin

3 sprigs fresh thyme, roughly chopped

½ Scotch bonnet pepper, julienned

1 white onion, thinly sliced

5 tablespoons canola oil

2 tablespoons fresh lime juice

3 tablespoons white rum (optional)

2 tablespoons all-purpose flour

1. Put the goat in a large mixing bowl and season with the salt, black pepper, allspice, coriander, paprika, red pepper flakes, garlic powder, 3 tablespoons curry powder, and the cumin and stir well to evenly coat all of the pieces.

2. Add the thyme, Scotch bonnet, onion, 2 tablespoons of the oil, and the lime juice and toss to coat. Cover and refrigerate overnight or for at least 2 hours to marinate.

3. Heat 3 tablespoons of the oil in a large Dutch oven or cast-iron pot over

high heat. When the oil is hot, add 2 tablespoons curry powder. Stirring continuously to avoid scorching, cook for 30 to 45 seconds.

4. Add the seasoned goat to the pot. Add flour, then pour 1 cup water into the seasoning bowl and stir until combined, scraping the sides, to mix in the leftover seasoning. Push the meat aside and pour in the seasoned slurry water carefully to avoid washing the seasoning off of the meat.

5. Reduce the heat to medium or medium-low and add rum if desired. Simmer for 2 hours or more, until tender. Serve.

Grilled Lamb Chops

BY CHEF IRIE

Grilling is a great way to cook lamb chops. After they've cooked through, drizzle them with Guava Mint Sauce (or any sauce that is sweet with a slight minty flavor). The lamb chops can be served by themselves or accompanied by mashed potatoes, risotto, vegetables, mashed broccoli, or cauliflower.

Serves 4 or 5

4 or 5 lamb chops

1½ teaspoons salt

1 teaspoon black pepper

1½ teaspoons red pepper flakes

2 teaspoons garlic powder

2 teaspoons ground coriander

3 tablespoons canola oil

1. Put the lamb chops in a large mixing bowl and season with the salt, black pepper, red pepper flakes, garlic powder, and coriander. Add 2 tablespoons of the oil and toss to coat. Cover and refrigerate for 20 minutes to 1 hour to marinate.

2. Lightly oil a grill grate and preheat the grill to high. When the grill is hot, carefully place the lamb chops on it and cook for 4 minutes, or until there are visible grill marks.

3. Flip the lamb chops and continue to cook for 3 to 4 minutes, to preferred doneness.

4. Serve drizzled with Guava Mint Sauce (page 56).

Glazed Pork Loin

BY CHEF IRIE

This is a straightforward recipe to which you can add any sauce of your choice. Be careful not to sear the pork too long or it will become overcooked. Try it with my Pineapple Sugarcane Glaze.

Serves 4

4 pork loins, about 6 ounces each

½ teaspoon salt

1 teaspoon black pepper

2 teaspoons garlic powder

2 teaspoons ground cumin

Canola oil for frying

1. Put the pork loins in a large mixing bowl and season with the salt, pepper, garlic powder, and cumin. Cover and refrigerate for 20 minutes to 1 hour to marinate.
2. Heat the oil in a large frying pan over medium-high heat. When the oil is hot, add the pork loin and sear for 3 to 4 minutes, or until white with browned edges. Flip the chops and sear for an additional 3 to 4 minutes.
3. Serve drizzled with Pineapple Sugarcane Glaze (page 68).

Pan-Grilled Jerk Pork Medallions

BY CHEF IRIE

Jerk pork is a big deal in Jamaica. They'll usually make it with robust cuts of pork, but I've used pork loin for a more refined presentation. I would pair this dish with rice, rice and peas, fried *bammy*, fried festival, or even a toasted, buttered bagel.

If you don't have an outdoor grill but do have an indoor grill pan, you can still get the same smokiness. Just make sure that your vent is on or a window is open, and be careful not to use too much of the jerk paste. Because of the amazing spices in the jerk, you may end up coughing or sneezing if your grilling area is not well ventilated.

Serves 4 to 6

2 pounds pork loin

For the Jerk Sauce

¼ cup chopped red bell pepper

¼ cup chopped green bell pepper

½ cup chopped yellow onion

3 teaspoons chopped fresh ginger

4 cloves garlic

2 to 5 whole Scotch bonnet peppers (adjust quantity for desired heat)

2 tablespoons brown sugar

1 tablespoon ground cinnamon

3 teaspoons ground allspice

1½ teaspoons grated nutmeg

¼ cup soy sauce

¼ cup canola oil

3 tablespoons Worcestershire sauce

1 teaspoon salt

¼ cup chopped fresh thyme on the stem

Juice of ½ lime

4 to 6 scallions, chopped

2 tablespoons dark Caribbean rum

2 teaspoons browning sauce

½ bunch fresh cilantro (optional)

1. Remove silverskin from the pork loin and cut the loin into 1-inch-thick medallions. Put in a large bowl.
2. Add all the jerk ingredients to a blender. Use one Scotch bonnet for mild flavor; as desired, add peppers to the mixture one by one to dial up the heat.
3. Blend the jerk ingredients together until completely pulverized.
4. Pour the jerk sauce over the pork loins, thoroughly covering the meat

with the sauce, and allow to marinate for at least 20 minutes but preferably in the refrigerator overnight.

5. Lightly wipe or spray a grill pan or grill grates with oil and preheat to high.

6. Scrape large chunks of the seasoning off the pork medallions to minimize burning before adding to the hot grill pan or grill.

7. Add only a few medallions to the grill at a time so as not to bring down the temperature of the grill or grill pan. For a crisscross grill pattern, after about 1 minute spin the pork 90 degrees on the same side.

8. Cook for a total of 3 to 4 minutes on each side. You'll know it's cooked when there's only a slight strip of bright pink left in the middle. If you leave it on the grill too long, it may become rubbery. Remove from the grill and allow to rest for a minute or two.

9. Slice the medallions and serve over rice or Herb Apple Salad (page 29). Smother with Mango Chutney (page 61) to balance heat with sweetness.

Chef Irie's tip: The seeds carry the heat of the peppers, so be very careful handling them. Do not touch your skin, eyes, or other sensitive body parts after touching peppers! If contact occurs, wash for a few minutes with cold water or milk.

Churrasco Beef with Chimichurri Sauce

BY CHEF THIA

My version of churrasco beef is straightforward and delicious. The steak is washed in sour orange juice and then grilled with salt and pepper, butter, and of course a little bit of Chef Thia's Spice. You want to use churrasco steak as opposed to a different cut, because it's fatty, flavorful, and perfect for grilling. This steak pairs perfectly with Chimichurri Sauce. When the acid from the sauce combines with the fat from the meat, it's like a flavor explosion.

Serves 4

1 (16-ounce) skirt (churrasco) steak

½ cup sour orange juice

1 teaspoon salt

¼ teaspoon black pepper

½ teaspoon red pepper flakes

3 tablespoons Chef Thia's Spice (page 66)

Chimichurri Sauce (page 71)

1. Put the steak in a large mixing bowl and pour the sour orange juice and ½ cup water over it. Allow to soak for 10 to 20 minutes, then drain the juice.

2. Season with the salt, black pepper, and red pepper flakes.

3. Preheat a grill to medium-high. When the grill grate is hot, carefully lay the steak on it, fat side down, and grill for 3 to 4 minutes.

4. Flip the steak and continue to cook for 3 minutes for medium steak, or up to 5 minutes for well-done.

5. Remove the steak from the grill and immediately spread the Chef Thia's Spice over the top. Allow it to soak in for 8 to 10 minutes before serving.

6. Serve with Chimichurri Sauce.

Carni Stoba (Stewed Beef)

BY CHEF IRIE

This is a meaty, savory dish from the Dutch Antilles. People in the ABC islands—Aruba, Bonaire, and Curaçao—absolutely love it, according to some college friends who hailed from there. It goes well served with roasted or mashed potatoes, rice, large-cut french fries, or cassava fries, and a nice light salad.

Serves 4 to 6

3 tablespoons canola oil

2 pounds beef sirloin, cut into 1-inch cubes

4 cloves garlic, thinly sliced

2 teaspoons browning sauce

3 tablespoons flour

1 teaspoon black pepper

1 teaspoon salt

2 teaspoons ground cumin

1 teaspoon grated nutmeg

½ cup thinly sliced white onion

½ cup sliced carrot

½ cup diced red bell pepper

½ cup diced green bell pepper

½ cup chopped tomatoes

2 cups diced potatoes

2 to 3 sprigs fresh thyme

1 tablespoon minced fresh ginger

3 tablespoons mushroom soy sauce

3 tablespoons Worcestershire sauce

3 tablespoons white wine

2 cups hot water or chicken or beef stock

2 cups cubed semi-ripe papaya

2 tablespoons tomato paste

1. Heat the oil in a large Dutch oven or cast-iron pot over medium-high heat. When the oil is hot, add the beef. Cook the beef for 3 to 5 minutes, stirring occasionally, until browned.

2. Add the garlic and browning sauce, then stir. Add the flour and stir in well.

3. Season with the black pepper, salt, and cumin and stir well. Continue to cook for 1 to 2 minutes.

4. Add the nutmeg, onion, carrot, and bell peppers and stir. Continue to cook for 2 to 3 minutes. If it isn't sizzling, increase the heat.

5. Add the tomatoes, potatoes, thyme, and ginger and stir. Continue to cook for 1 to 2 minutes.

6. Add the mushroom soy sauce and Worcestershire sauce and stir. Then stir in the wine. Continue to cook for 1 to 2 minutes.

7. Add the hot water, stir, and cover the pot. Cook for 15 minutes.

8. While the stew is cooking, steam the papaya over medium heat for 10 to 15 minutes, or until tender, but not mushy.

9. Add the steamed papaya and the tomato paste to the stew and gently stir. Lower the heat to medium and simmer for 5 minutes. Serve.

Picadillo Meatballs

BY CHEF IRIE

Picadillo is a Cuban ground beef dish made with olives, raisins, and seasonings. The obvious question that led to the creation of this dish was—why make a regular meatball when you can make it with picadillo? Serve it over rice, plantains, or pasta.

Make sure that the meatballs are completely chilled before cooking. This step will help them hold together during the cooking process.

Serves 4

For the Meatballs

1½ pounds ground beef (sirloin, chuck, or a combination of both)

½ pound ground chorizo or pork

½ cup finely diced smoked ham

¼ cup finely diced green bell pepper

¼ cup finely diced red bell pepper

¼ cup green olives, chopped

½ cup golden raisins, chopped

¼ cup diced red pimiento

4 cloves garlic, chopped

2 teaspoons red pepper flakes

¼ cup chopped fresh cilantro

¼ cup chopped fresh flat-leaf parsley leaves

3 scallions, chopped

¼ cup finely diced yellow onion

1 tablespoon fresh thyme leaves

2 tablespoons dry adobo seasoning

3 tablespoons Worcestershire sauce

3 tablespoons olive oil

1 egg, beaten

¾ cup panko bread crumbs

2 tablespoons paprika

1 teaspoon cayenne pepper

2 tablespoons ground cumin

1 tablespoon ground oregano

For the Tomato Basil Sauce

2 tablespoons olive oil

½ cup chopped onion

3 cloves chopped garlic

2 cups chopped tomatoes

2 cups tomato sauce

4 cups chicken or vegetable stock

1 teaspoon red pepper flakes

1 tablespoon adobo seasoning

½ bunch fresh basil, stems removed

1 teaspoon chopped fresh ginger

1 teaspoon kosher salt

1 teaspoon black pepper

2 tablespoons tomato paste

1. Make the meatballs: Put the beef and chorizo in a large bowl and then add all the remaining ingredients. Using clean hands, mix until everything is thoroughly combined. Remove and form into medium-size balls. Refrigerate for about 30 minutes.

2. Make the tomato basil sauce: Put the oil in a medium stockpot over medium heat. Add the onion and garlic and cook for about 30 seconds. Add the tomatoes and remaining ingredients. Allow to come to a simmer.

3. Use a hand blender to puree the tomato mixture until almost smooth. Check the seasoning and adjust the salt and pepper to taste.

4. Add the chilled meatballs one at a time. Give a quick, gentle stir. Cover the pot and reduce the heat to a gentle simmer and cook for about 45 minutes. Serve.

Chef Irie's tip: To check desired seasoning in the meatball mixture, cook a small sample in a frying pan before chilling the mixture and taste before forming the meat into balls.

Photograph by Nicole Hylton Richards.

Steak Roulade

BY CHEF THIA

My steak roulade is a thin marinated steak, rolled with scallions and sweet bell peppers, sautéed, and finished in the oven. Serve it with Parmesan-topped french fries—amazing!

The thinner your steak, the better.

Serves 2

1 pound *palomilla* steak, in two portions

2 tablespoons olive oil

1 teaspoon Worcestershire sauce

1 teaspoon soy sauce

2 tablespoons red wine vinegar

1 tablespoon fresh thyme leaves

1 teaspoon red pepper flakes

½ red bell pepper, sliced

½ orange bell pepper, sliced

¼ green bell pepper, sliced

¼ yellow bell pepper, sliced

2 scallions, cut in half

Supplies

4 to 6 toothpicks or short wooden skewers

1. Soak wooden skewers for at least 10 minutes to avoid splintering while grilling.

2. In a medium bowl, mix all the ingredients except the bell peppers and scallions together and allow the meat to marinate for 1 hour.

3. Moisten 3 slices red pepper, 2 slices orange pepper, 1 slice green pepper, 1 slice yellow pepper, and a piece of scallion in the marinade, then wrap them with one of the steak portions and roll into a tight log. Skewer with 2 or 3 toothpicks or wooden skewer sticks to hold together. Repeat with the remaining vegetables and steak.

4. Preheat a grill or oiled grill pan to high. Place the steak roulades on the hot grate or pan and grill for 5 to 7 minutes on each side.

5. Remove from the grill and allow the roulades to rest for 1 minute before slicing into 1-inch pieces. Serve hot.

6

Sides

Many Caribbean side dishes share common ancestry. With the advent of the slave trade in the fifteenth century, cheap, filling food offerings were sought out for sustenance. Some of these foods, brought by the Europeans and the slaves, were introduced into the tropical ecosystem and still survive today.

Rice, native to the East, is one of those foods that have survived. It is safe to say that regardless of whether you're looking at English, French, Spanish, or Dutch Caribbean islands, all maintain a love affair with rice, the second greatest source of calories in the region behind sugar. Many of the islands combine rice with beans, in dishes that may or may not include coconut milk or spices and seasonings. It is notable that although they may look the same, you might be enjoying "rice and peas" or "peas and rice" depending on where you are and who you're asking. You'll find popular one-pot rice meals that incorporate legumes and proteins, like Latin Caribbean arroz con pollo and paella, and Trinidadian *pelau*, which Chef Irie explored in the previous chapter.

Cornmeal has also endured as an inexpensive but filling food element. From Latin polenta, which Chef Thia includes in her recipe mix, to Barbadian *coucou*, which Chef Irie makes, there's a selection of flavorful, soft polenta-like dishes to choose from. Jamaicans also use cornmeal to make a fried sweet bread called festival, which is a popular companion to fried snapper or jerk chicken on the island.

Provisions like yams, breadfruit, cassava, bananas, and plantains—whole foods from the ground, tree, or vine that can be cooked and eaten without necessarily being combined with anything else—largely came from Africa and the East. They're still commonly eaten throughout the region, simply boiled, roasted, baked, or fried in their natural state, sometimes with a bit of salt. You'll also find them made into cakes and chips. In modern gourmet fare, however, these elements can be prepared in far more intriguing ways. See Chef Irie's Mashed Yellow Yam and his Breadfruit Pumpkin Salad, for example.

You'll be able to find most of these ingredients in a local ethnic store, wherever you are. Enjoy!

Camarofongo (Smashed Plantains)

BY CHEF IRIE

This preparation is one way to transform the hard and starchy plantain into a soft dish infused with flavors. You can keep it simple with salt and pepper, add seasonings, or even add some meat. The texture should be soft and lumpy and slightly grainy, almost like rustic mashed potatoes. Serve with Creole Shrimp (page 74) or pair it with breakfast food like eggs or Ackee and Saltfish (page 98).

Serves 4

2 large green (unripe) plantains

3 tablespoons unsalted butter, softened

¼ cup coconut milk

½ teaspoon kosher salt

½ teaspoon black pepper

1 teaspoon ground cumin

3 teaspoons garlic powder

2 teaspoons dried oregano

2 tablespoons chopped fresh cilantro

1. Peel and chop the plantains into chunks. Add to boiling salted water and boil for 15 to 20 minutes, until fork tender. Drain and return the plantains to the pot.
2. Add the butter, coconut milk, salt, pepper, cumin, garlic powder, oregano, and cilantro and mash until smooth, then serve.

Grilled Plantains

BY CHEF IRIE

Plantains are such a versatile fruit, and grilling is a delicious way to enjoy them. These grilled plantains can be paired with saltfish or jerk chicken and vegetables such as callaloo, spinach, or sautéed cabbage. Use plantains that are ripened enough to have a little give when pressed firmly. Plantains that are underripe will not grill nicely.

Serves 4

2 large medium-ripe plantains

2 tablespoons canola oil

½ teaspoon salt

½ teaspoon black pepper

Chadon Beni Sauce (page 57)

1. Peel and slice the plantains in half lengthwise and crosswise, and brush with canola oil. Then sprinkle on both sides with salt and pepper.
2. Preheat a grill to high. Grill the plantain slices for 5 to 8 minutes, or until there are grill marks. Flip and continue to grill for 3 to 4 minutes.
3. Drizzle with sauce and serve.

Grilled French Baguette

BY CHEF IRIE

This is another simple side to serve with any stew, chowder, or soup.

Serves 8

1 loaf French baguette

¼ cup olive oil

1 teaspoon red pepper flakes

1 teaspoon garlic powder

½ teaspoon kosher salt

1. Heat a grill to medium.
2. Cut the baguette diagonally into 1-inch-thick slices.
3. Mix the remaining ingredients together in a small bowl, brush on both sides of the baguette slices, and grill until golden, about 4 minutes on each side.
4. Serve with my Mussels Chorizo in Mango Coconut Sauce (page 81) or other entrée.

Mashed Yellow Yam

BY CHEF IRIE

I grew up eating ground provisions like different types of yams, but always had them boiled in cubes or roasted. I realized that as a starch, yams could certainly be mashed. Serve them as you would any starchy side—they go well with seafood or steak, or with other vegetables.

Be sure to mash only until they're a little fluffy and lumpy; if overmashed, yams can become a little too starchy. You could use malanga, yuca, boniatos, or any other kind of firm yam instead of the yellow yam if it is not available.

Serves 4 to 6

1 tablespoon fresh lime juice

4 cups peeled and chopped yellow yam

½ teaspoon salt

¼ teaspoon black pepper

3 tablespoons unsalted butter

½ cup coconut milk

1. Rub the lime juice on the yam to prevent discoloration.
2. Bring a large pot of water to a boil over medium-high heat. Add the yam and boil for 20 to 30 minutes, until they are tender. Drain.
3. Add the yam, salt, pepper, butter, and coconut milk to a food processor and pulse to a slightly chunky texture. Serve warm.

Coucou

BY CHEF IRIE

Throughout the islands there are slightly different versions of this dish with different names; *coucou* is the Barbados style usually served with flying fish, but in Jamaica it's called turned cornmeal, and on several other islands it's called *fungi*. *Coucou* goes well with almost anything but is also a great dish all by itself. Pair it with meat, seafood, vegetables, shredded pork, shredded chicken, or shrimp or cook any of these right into the *coucou*.

You want to use medium or fine cornmeal, not coarse, because the consistency once it is done should be smooth. Allow it to firm up in a bowl so that when it is put on the plate it will have the form of the bowl.

Serves 8

1 teaspoon salt	4 large okra pods, thinly sliced
½ teaspoon black pepper	6 sprigs fresh thyme
½ teaspoon Cajun seasoning	2 tablespoons unsalted butter
¼ cup diced yellow onion	½ cup diced tomatoes
1 large clove garlic, diced	1¼ cups medium-ground cornmeal
½ Scotch bonnet pepper, diced	Olive oil

1. In a large stockpot, combine 4 cups water and all the remaining ingredients except the cornmeal and oil and bring to a boil. Reduce the heat to medium and cook for about 10 minutes to allow flavors to steep into the water.

2. Remove the thyme and reduce the heat to low, then add the cornmeal a little at a time while continuously stirring. As the cornmeal starts to expand and the mixture thickens, stir vigorously until it starts to separate from the sides of the pot.

3. Brush the inside of a small bowl with oil, and spoon the mixture in, then smooth the top and invert into a plate.

4. Serve with my Escoveitch Fish (page 95) or other entrée.

Olympic Bites

We're fans of troublemakers and fun times on the set of *Taste the Islands*. Olympian and sports analyst Ato Boldon fit right in. Claiming that he was skilled enough to burn water, he came on set excited to wear an apron and impress his family, who would no doubt be incredulous that we got him into one.

Ato shared stories of growing up in Trinidad, eating "wild meat" like iguana, frequently having typical Trinidadian cuisine like roti, curries, and pepper chows—and like his countrymen, putting ketchup on everything, even pizza! During his career as a sprinter he was, of course, more careful about what he ate. After retiring from competitive athletics, however, he had become a little chubbier, confessing to Chef Irie that the temptation had become too strong, and without the fitness obligations of his previous career, he had immediately gone on a donut binge.

Now that he has rediscovered balance, he follows a healthier diet that still mixes in some of the more indulgent foods from his home country. Chef Irie invited Ato into his outdoor kitchen to prepare a deep-fried Trinidadian decadence: bake and shark. Although Ato

Ato Boldon, Chef Irie, and Lukkee Chong (*left to right*). Photograph by Nicole Hylton Richards.

wasn't a huge fan of heat, Chef Irie's spicy Mango Ketchup made the dish unique, without an overpowering pepper factor.

Try the combination of fried corvina, Trinidadian Bakes, Red Cabbage Slaw, and Mango Ketchup for yourself, or put some other protein you might like into the warm, crunchy pocket of Trinidadian Bakes. There's just so much you can do with these simple Caribbean meal elements. Enjoy! ☀

Top: Ato Boldon and Chef Irie. *Bottom*: Ato Boldon, Calibe Thompson, and Chef Irie. Photographs by Nicole Hylton Richards.

Trinidadian Bakes

BY CHEF IRIE

Bakes, a Trinidadian fried bread, are light and fluffy and hollow in the middle, making them great for sandwiches. They're especially popular in Trinidad for the dish called bake and shark. I was inspired to make these after experiencing bake and shark at carnival in Trinidad.

A good bake has the right fluffiness, crunchiness, and size. Make just one bake first to ensure that the oil is the right temperature, around 350°F, not too hot. If the oil is too hot, the bakes may overcook on the outside and be raw in the middle. When you're sure the temperature is right, you want to cook several bakes at a time to regulate the temperature of the oil. Fry until they are nice and golden brown on each side, then serve them warm.

Serves 3 to 4

2 cups all-purpose flour, plus extra for rolling

1 tablespoon baking powder

1 teaspoon granulated sugar

½ teaspoon salt

1 teaspoon unsalted butter, cut into cubes

2 cups canola oil

1. In a medium bowl, combine the flour, baking powder, sugar, and salt. Add the butter and mix until the texture resembles breadcrumbs.

2. Make a well in the center of the flour mixture and slowly pour in ¾ cup water while mixing. Add a little more water, if needed, to make a firm dough.

3. Knead the dough on a floured surface for about 5 minutes. If the dough is a little sticky, knead in an extra tablespoon of flour. Form the dough into a ball and place back in the bowl.

4. Brush the dough ball with a little oil and cover the bowl with a damp towel or plastic wrap. Allow to rest for 30 minutes.

Photograph by Nicole Hylton Richards.

5. On a well-floured surface, cut the dough evenly into 6 to 8 pieces and roll each piece into a ball. Cover with a damp towel or plastic wrap for 10 minutes.

6. Roll each dough ball to about ¼ inch thick and 5 to 6 inches across.

7. Heat the oil in a frying pan to 350°F. Without overcrowding the pan, carefully lay the dough into the hot oil. Fry each side for 30 to 45 seconds, until golden brown, all the while scooping oil over the tops. Place the bakes on paper towels to drain and cool a little.

8. To serve, cut each bake open to form a pocket, drizzle the inside with Mango Ketchup (page 65) and fill with Red Cabbage Slaw (page 23) and Chef Irie's Trini Shark (page 97).

Boniato Balls Sautéed with Onions

BY CHEF THIA

Boniatos and red onions are naturally sweet, plus this recipe has a little brown sugar in it. The sweetness is balanced with a touch of saltiness from the butter, creating a dish of pure deliciousness.

Make sure to boil the boniatos only until cooked but still firm. When you stick a knife into the boniato, it should go in easily but not break it apart. I like to use the small boniatos, which only take 20 to 40 minutes to cook. If you can't find boniatos, sweet potatoes can be used as a substitute. If you use sweet potatoes, cook them only until al dente or they'll break apart in the pan.

Serves 4

1½ pounds fresh boniatos

5 tablespoons unsalted butter

3 teaspoons brown sugar

1 teaspoon dark Caribbean rum

1½ cups sliced red onions

1. In a large pot of water, boil the boniatos whole until they are slightly softened but still a bit firm, about 40 minutes for large ones. Drain, cool, and peel.
2. Use a watermelon baller or spoon and scoop to form 1-inch balls of cooked boniato. This process should yield 10 to 15 balls.
3. Heat a frying pan over medium-high heat and add the butter and brown sugar. Once the butter is melted and the sugar has dissolved, add the rum, then add the onions and sauté until they become translucent and begin to release liquid.
4. Add the boniato balls and stir carefully to coat them with the butter and sugar. Cook for 3 to 5 minutes, gently stirring, until lightly browned. Serve warm.

Polenta with Spinach

BY CHEF THIA

I got my children to eat spinach with this recipe. Caribbean polenta has many variations and you can find it with almost anything mixed in. I make it very garlicky, so you don't even taste the spinach. If you love corn, this recipe is amazing! Serve this polenta with a good Haitian black bean sauce and avocado salad.

You don't want it to be clumpy, so pour the polenta into the pot very slowly with one hand while stirring constantly with the other.

Serves 4

6 tablespoons unsalted butter

⅔ cup finely chopped onion

1 scallion, finely chopped

2 Roma tomatoes, diced

2 tablespoons garlic paste

2 teaspoons salt

1½ cups polenta-style cornmeal (coarse yellow)

1 cup chopped spinach

Grated Parmesan cheese to taste (optional)

1. Heat a saucepan over medium-high heat and add 3 tablespoons of the butter. Add the onion and scallion and cook until translucent, about 1 minute.

2. Add the tomatoes and garlic paste and stir until the tomatoes start changing color, about 2 minutes.

3. Add 6 cups water and bring to a boil.

4. As the water is boiling, add the salt, then add the cornmeal gradually while stirring to ensure there are no lumps. Stir until smooth, then add the remaining 3 tablespoons butter.

5. Continue stirring until the water is absorbed and the mixture begins to bubble and thicken.

6. Reduce the heat to low, cover, and simmer for about 25 minutes, stirring every 5 minutes, until the water is almost completely absorbed.

7. Add the spinach in the last few minutes and stir.

8. While the polenta is hot, serve in a bowl. Add cheese upon plating, if desired.

Chef Thia's tip: You can also allow the polenta to cool and harden in a bowl or deep dish. You can then cut it and serve it warmed or at room temperature as a soft, al dente side.

Djon-Djon Mushroom Rice

BY CHEF THIA

My version of *djon-djon* rice has a fluffy texture and features Chef Thia's Spice, peas, and fresh mushrooms. Serve this with good seafood and some sauce or gravy.

You can use lima beans instead of peas, which is a popular variation of this dish. Sometimes I add shrimp, which tastes amazing. If you can't find *djon-djon* mushrooms, you can use squid or octopus ink for the dark color.

Serves 12

2 cups dried *djon-djon* mushrooms

1½ tablespoons salt

4 tablespoons canola oil

⅔ cup sliced bacon

⅔ cup diced red bell pepper

3 tablespoons Chef Thia's Spice
  (page 66)

2 cups frozen green peas or lima
  beans, thawed

3 cups parboiled basmati rice,
  rinsed

4 tablespoons unsalted butter

1 Scotch bonnet pepper, uncut

5 sprigs fresh thyme

1. Add the mushrooms to a large pot with 9 cups water and the salt and bring to a boil. Reduce the heat and simmer for 10 minutes, then remove from the heat.
2. Pour the mushrooms and liquid into a blender. Hold the lid tightly in place with a dish towel to protect your hand from the heat, and blend on high speed until liquefied.
3. Strain through a fine strainer, pressing the mushroom dregs through, and discard the solids in the strainer.
4. Heat the oil in a Dutch oven over medium-high heat. When the oil is hot, add the bacon, stirring until bacon starts to turn brown. Add the bell pepper and stir until it starts to change color, about 2 minutes.
5. Add the Chef Thia's Spice and stir for another 5 minutes until it starts to turn brown.
6. Add the peas and stir until thoroughly mixed with the seasoning.
7. Add 4¼ cups of the mushroom water skimmed from the top, and bring to a boil.

8. Add the rice and boil over high heat until the liquid is almost completely absorbed. Lower the heat to medium so the rice doesn't begin to burn.

9. Add the butter and mix everything together until the rice is completely dry. Add the uncut Scotch bonnet and the thyme on top of the rice.

10. Cover and reduce the heat to low. Cook for 25 to 30 minutes until rice is soft. Stir to ensure the seasoning settled on the bottom is distributed all the way through.

11. Serve with your favorite protein.

Chef Thia's tip: Garnish the rice with julienned fresh Scotch bonnet pepper to add extra sizzle.

Vegetarian Legume

BY CHEF THIA

Legume is a traditional Haitian dish which I have modified for my friends who do not eat meat. This vegetarian version is light, leafy, and very flavorful with eggplant, chayote, and spinach. Serve with good jasmine rice—it's an amazing vegetable parade!

Everyone does legume a different way. People usually include a combination of okra, crabmeat, seafood, pork, and/or beef; I usually like to add seafood and beef. Add any of these to your legume and enjoy experimenting!

Serves 4 to 6

⅓ cup olive oil

2 yellow onions, diced

3 Roma tomatoes, diced

1 cup finely diced red bell pepper

½ cup finely diced green bell pepper

3 ribs celery with leaves on, finely diced

½ head of cabbage, shredded

½ cup Chef Thia's Spice (page 66)

1 cup dry white wine

1½ teaspoons lemon pepper seasoned salt

1½ teaspoons complete seasoning (or all-purpose seasoning)

3 to 4 vegetable bouillon cubes (optional)

1 tablespoon Himalayan pink salt

1 teaspoon black pepper

1 large eggplant, diced

2 tablespoons tomato paste

1½ cups vegetable stock

6 sprigs fresh thyme

1 whole Scotch bonnet pepper

2 large carrots

2 packed cups chopped spinach

2 tablespoons unsalted butter

1 cup frozen green peas, thawed

1. Heat the oil in a large Dutch oven or stockpot over medium-high heat. When the oil is hot, add the onions and stir until translucent, 2 to 3 minutes.
2. Add the tomatoes and stir until they start to change color.
3. Add the bell peppers, celery, and cabbage and mix well.
4. Add the Chef Thia's Spice, wine, lemon pepper seasoned salt, complete seasoning, bouillon cubes (if using), salt, and black pepper and stir together. Lower the heat to medium-low and simmer for 5 minutes.

5. Add the eggplant, tomato paste, and stock and mix together. Place the thyme and whole Scotch bonnet on top of the mixture, then cover the pot and lower the heat to simmer for 25 minutes.

6. Add the carrots and mix in, being careful not to break the Scotch bonnet. Simmer for another 30 minutes.

7. Remove from the heat and add the spinach, butter, and peas. Let stand for 5 to 10 minutes.

8. Serve with boiled yam, boiled potatoes, or white rice.

Roasted Potato Slices

BY CHEF THIA

I came up with this recipe one day when I needed to make something quick and happened to have some potatoes, garlic, and butter on hand—all things that I love. These roasted potato slices are crispy and full of flavor. Enjoy them alone as a snack, or with a nice steak or fish.

Two handfuls of sliced fingerling potatoes are a great option for this recipe.

Serves 2

2 medium roasting potatoes

Salt

⅔ cup chopped fresh curly parsley

4 cloves garlic, roughly chopped

⅛ teaspoon paprika

Zest of ½ lemon

1 tablespoon fresh rosemary leaves, roughly chopped

4 tablespoons olive oil

⅛ teaspoon black pepper

1. Cut the potatoes into ¼-inch-thick wedges. Add some salt to a bowl of water, then soak the potato wedges in the salted water for 2 hours to marinate, then drain and return the potatoes to the bowl.

2. Preheat the oven to 350°F. Line a rimmed baking sheet with parchment paper.

3. Add the parsley, garlic, paprika, lemon zest, rosemary, oil, pepper, and ½ teaspoon salt to the bowl with the drained potato wedges, then mix gently together until the potatoes are completely coated.

4. Spread on the baking sheet.

5. Bake for 20 minutes, or until golden brown.

6. Serve with Red Snapper Fillet (page 88) or another entrée.

7

Desserts

Desserts that originate in the Caribbean truly reflect the mix of cultures in the region. They incorporate local fruit and produce to make sweets that are simply and tropically delightful.

Where there is a strong African influence, the desserts lean toward being a little bit more firm or substantial, incorporating grains and ground provisions, while the desserts influenced by Latin and French cultures tend to be lighter and fluffier.

Visit Jamaica and you'll find desserts like *toto*—a sweet and solid coconut bread; bread pudding, often with rum and raisins in the mix; sweet potato pudding—a heavy, dark, smoothly textured cake with boniatos (Caribbean sweet potatoes) as the main ingredient; coconut drops—similar to brittle, but softer and made with chunks of dried coconut; and plantain tarts—sweet plantains mashed and baked inside a pastry puff. These tend to be heavier and more filling.

Hop over to the Latin islands and you'll find sweeter, more velvety options like flan—a gelatinous pudding made with sweetened condensed milk; *tres leches*—a tender white cake with soft icing and a sweet, creamy sauce; *tembleque*—a delicate coconut pudding; flaky *pasteles* stuffed with guava and/or cheese and other light delights. Latin chefs are extremely adept at incorporating tropical ingredients like mango, guava, passion fruit, and mamey into jellies, mousses, and ice creams as well.

Many islands enjoy slightly varied versions of nut brittles, coconut bread, rum cakes, and bread puddings. Cooking techniques like wrapping and steaming in banana leaves transcend items like Latin tamales, St. Lucian duckunoo, and Barbadian conkies.

A common holiday dessert is Christmas pudding or "black cake," a British import that includes a baked or steamed mix of liquor-soaked dried fruit. Other holiday treats include the aforementioned conkies and duckunoo, as well as the fairly ubiquitous rum cake. These will be served with sorrel and *ponche crema*, *coquito*, or *cremas*, which we'll learn more about in the drinks section.

Our chefs have chosen just a few of these recipes to share, in both their traditional formats, like Chef Thia's Pain Patate (Sweet Potato Pudding), or in their own deconstructed format, like Chef Irie's Guava Cream Cheese Phyllo Tartlets. Some of these desserts, such as the Molten Apple Noodle Cakes, are unique creations you'll likely not find anywhere else. Enjoy!

Molten Apple Noodle Cakes

BY CHEF IRIE

I call this dessert "apple pie meets funnel cake." This dish combines noodle cakes—my take on funnel cakes found at county fairs—with a deconstructed apple pie that is flavored with Caribbean rum and dessert spices.

You can use spaghetti noodles or ramen noodles, but you don't want to use noodles like angel hair, which are too thin.

Serves 4

For the Apple Compote

3 cups sliced Granny Smith apples

⅓ cup orange juice

1 cup (2 sticks) unsalted butter

1 teaspoon grated nutmeg

3 teaspoons ground cinnamon

2 teaspoons ground ginger

½ cup sugar

2 teaspoons vanilla extract

2 tablespoons dark Caribbean rum

¼ cup peanut butter

½ teaspoon salt

For the Noodle Cakes

2 cups lo mein noodles or cooked spaghetti

Canola oil for frying

1 tablespoon sugar

1 teaspoon ground cinnamon

1 teaspoon grated nutmeg

1. Make the apple compote: Put the apple slices in a medium bowl and pour the orange juice over them. Toss the apples and set aside.

2. Melt the butter in a frying pan over medium heat. Add the nutmeg, cinnamon, ginger, sugar, vanilla, and rum and stir well. Reserving the orange juice, add the apple slices to the pan and stir to coat them evenly.

3. Add the peanut butter to the orange juice and stir to break up any large clumps (it will be a little lumpy). Pour the mixture over the apples, stir, and sprinkle with the salt. Simmer for 20 minutes.

4. Make the noodle cakes: If using lo mein noodles, cook them in boiling water

for about 5 minutes, drain, and set aside. If using spaghetti, cook in boiling water until al dente, 8 to 10 minutes, drain, and set aside.

5. Heat oil in a small frying pan over medium-high heat to a temperature of 350°F.

6. When the oil is hot, add a nest of noodles (using ¼ of the noodles) to the pan and fry for 2 to 3 minutes, until golden brown on one side. Flip the noodles and continue to fry for an additional 1 to 2 minutes. Remove the noodle cake from the oil and place on paper towels to drain. Immediately sprinkle with sugar, cinnamon, and nutmeg. Repeat with the remaining noodles, for a total of four noodle cakes.

7. To serve, place noodle cakes on individual serving plates and smother with the warm apple compote.

Guava Cream Cheese Phyllo Tartlets

BY CHEF IRIE

My starting point here is *pasteles*, Cuban-style treats. Instead of putting guava and cream cheese in a puff pastry, like they do in Cuban culture, I decided to make a filling that could be put inside a phyllo "nest." The filling is very creamy and only moderately sweet.

I definitely recommend using a food processor to make the filling. Also make sure you don't overcook the phyllo dough. It should be slightly golden brown.

Serves 12

6 sheets phyllo dough

8 ounces guava paste

1 pound softened cream cheese

4 tablespoons dark Caribbean rum

3 tablespoons orange juice

¼ teaspoon ground cinnamon

½ cup melted unsalted butter

2 tablespoons sugar

Fresh basil leaves, julienned

1. Preheat the oven to 375°F. Thaw the phyllo dough according to the package instructions.

2. Put the guava paste, cream cheese, rum, orange juice, and cinnamon in a food processor or blender and puree until smooth. Transfer to a bowl, cover, and place in the refrigerator to chill.

3. Brush butter over one sheet of phyllo, lay another sheet on top, and repeat to make a stack of three. Repeat this process with the remaining three sheets. Sprinkle sugar over the phyllo.

4. Cut the layered phyllo sheets into 4-inch squares. Gently press each square into a regular muffin tin.

5. Bake for 8 to 10 minutes, until lightly browned. Allow to cool completely.

6. To serve, scoop guava filling into the phyllo crisps and garnish with basil.

Photograph by Nicole Hylton Richards.

Photograph by Nicole Hylton Richards.

Mango Key Lime Pie

BY CHEF IRIE

Key lime pies were made famous down in the Florida Keys, where that fruit primarily grows. Living in South Florida, I wanted make my own version of a Key lime pie. I am always combining fruit components, so I decided to add a tropical fruit that I love, mango. The tartness of the Key lime balances so nicely with the sweetness of the mango!

Serves 8

5 egg yolks

14 ounces sweetened condensed milk

½ cup fresh Key lime juice

1 ripe mango, diced

1 teaspoon vanilla extract

1 tablespoon dark Caribbean rum (optional)

1 packaged graham cracker crust

Whipped cream (optional)

Fresh mango slices (optional)

Key lime slices (optional)

1. Preheat the oven to 325°F.

2. Use an electric mixer to beat the egg yolks and condensed milk until smooth. Add the Key lime juice, mango, vanilla, and rum, and continue to beat until mostly smooth (the mango chunks should break down a little, but not completely).

3. Pour the mixture into the pie crust until nearly full. Gently shake the pie back and forth to make the filling level.

4. Bake for 25 to 35 minutes, until the filling springs back gently to the touch. Allow to cool, then refrigerate until chilled.

5. Serve topped with whipped cream and fresh mango and garnished with Key lime slices, if desired.

Passion Fruit Mousse

BY CHEF IRIE

Whipped cream mousse recipes often incorporate a fruit flavor, so I chose to use passion fruit. Passion fruit has a strong tanginess that definitely requires something sweet to temper it.

You don't want to overwhip the whipped cream because it might become grainy and break down. Whip the cream until it just forms stiff peaks on the blade of the mixer, then gently fold in the passion fruit puree in batches.

Serves 4

1½ cups passion fruit puree

¼ cup sugar

⅛ teaspoon salt

1 pint heavy cream

Rum, vanilla extract, or ground cloves (optional)

1. Place a metal bowl or stand mixer bowl in the freezer for 30 minutes.

2. In a small bowl, combine the passion fruit puree, sugar, and salt and stir.

3. Add the cream to the chilled bowl and beat with an electric mixer on medium speed until it has thickened.

4. Gently fold the passion fruit mixture into the cream. A small amount of rum, vanilla, or a pinch of ground cloves may be added, if desired.

5. Cover the bowl and refrigerate to chill before serving.

Photograph by Nicole Hylton Richards.

Rum and Raisin Bread Pudding

BY CHEF IRIE

Rum and raisins are very common in Caribbean desserts. I like to taste the rum in my food, so I cook with rum a lot. Infusing it into this bread pudding reminded me of the way we do it at home in Jamaica. Rum adds a caramel flavor, sweetness, and smokiness. This is otherwise a classic bread pudding, so of course it's nice and soft.

Serves 8 to 10

6 tablespoons raisins

¼ cup dark Caribbean rum

6 eggs

2 teaspoons grated nutmeg

2 teaspoons ground cinnamon

2 teaspoons ground ginger

3 teaspoons vanilla extract

1 teaspoon rosewater

¾ cup heavy cream

2½ cups coconut milk

½ teaspoon salt

4 tablespoons unsalted butter, melted

1½ cups brown sugar

6 cups large-cubed challah or Italian bread, with crust

1. Preheat the oven to 325°F.
2. In a small bowl, soak the raisins in the rum to hydrate.
3. In a large bowl, whisk the eggs, and then whisk in the spices, vanilla, rosewater, cream, coconut milk, salt, butter, and brown sugar. Once liquids and spices have been completely combined, add the bread squares and mix together gently, without pulverizing the cubes, until the bread has been completely saturated. Add the raisins and rum and mix in until raisins are evenly distributed.
4. Grease the bottom and sides of a 9 by 13-inch baking pan with butter, then add the bread pudding mixture. Bake for 30 minutes, or until a toothpick or knife inserted comes out dry. Serve warm, with Coconut Custard Sauce (page 184) if desired.

Sweet Sugar Dumpling

Rory Lee has been a friend of *Taste the Islands* since the beginning. As a Bahamian American woman in the world of film and television, she is proud of the work we are doing in putting the show together and featuring Caribbean culture. She lends her support whenever possible, including helping us out with our on-set makeup and hair in season 2. When we invited her to step in front of the camera for a segment, she was thrilled to be a part of it.

It was Chef Thia's vegetarian episode featuring some yummy meat-free dishes, mostly made in the Haitian style. Rory commented that the refreshing Raw Vegan Salad, made with pear, carrots, and chayote, reminded her of a special dessert more than something healthy. But the dish that captured all our attention was the Pain Patate. Jamaicans have their own version of this boniato (Caribbean sweet potato) pudding, but Thia's very similar dish includes ripe bananas cooked first on the stove, and then baked in little ramekins for a delightful presentation. Upon further investigation, we learned that the Latin community uses sweet potatoes to make a boniato dessert with a more cake-like consistency, and the Barbadian version of sweet potato pudding is actually a savory side that they serve with a pickled pork dish called souse. Following this pudding across so many islands still stands as one of our favorite learning moments! ☀

Rory Lee, Chef Thia, Lisa Lee Arneaud, Calibe Thompson, and Lukkee Chong (*left to right*).

Adam Heim, Tyler Council, Rory Lee, Chef Thia, Lukkee Chong, Lisa Lee Arneaud, Calibe Thompson, and Brandon Mitchell (*left to right*).

Pain Patate (Sweet Potato Pudding)

BY CHEF THIA

My version of this classic Haitian dish is a lot quicker and easier than traditional recipes, but with the same flavor and texture. It's soft and mildly sweet with the flavors of coconut, rum, and butter. It's just amazing. You can pulverize the boniato more easily with a food processor, but a good old grater does the trick just as well. You'll just need a lot more elbow grease.

Serves 6

¾ cup (1½ sticks) unsalted butter

6 cups peeled and grated boniatos

2 cups coconut milk

2 bananas, thinly sliced

⅔ cup brown sugar

1 teaspoon ground cinnamon

¼ teaspoon grated nutmeg

1 (13-ounce) can sweetened condensed milk

1 tablespoon vanilla extract

1 cup sweetened coconut flakes

5 pods star anise

¼ teaspoon salt

1 cup raisins

¼ cup dark Caribbean rum

1. Melt the butter in a large Dutch oven or heavy stockpot over medium-high heat. Add the boniatos, then stir in the coconut milk 1 cup at a time.
2. Add the bananas and crush until melted, then reduce the heat to medium-low.
3. Add the brown sugar, cinnamon, nutmeg, condensed milk, vanilla, and coconut flakes and stir for at least 5 minutes, until the boniatos begin to caramelize.
4. Add the star anise and salt, stirring continuously. When the mixture begins to thicken and become sticky, mix in the raisins and rum until combined. Remove from the heat and allow to sit for 30 minutes.
5. Preheat the oven to 350°F. Grease a 9 by 13-inch baking pan.
6. Remove the star anise and add the boniato mixture to the prepared baking pan. Bake for 40 minutes. Serve warm or cool.

Pear and Pineapple Flambé

BY CHEF THIA

Flambé is the French technique of setting food on fire with drinking alcohol as the accelerant. I incorporated tropical fruit and Caribbean dark rum for this delightful dessert.

Some tips for the flambé process: Be very careful and don't try this under a microwave hood, near curtains, or near anything flammable. Also, don't put out the fire in the pan, just wait and it will go out on its own. Stand back when you add the rum; you don't want to get burned! Don't try this with kids around.

Serves 2

6 tablespoons unsalted butter

4 round slices pineapple, cored

½ pear, cut lengthwise into 8 slices

⅔ cup sugar

½ cup dark Caribbean rum (strong)

2 fresh mint leaves, chopped

1. In a medium pan over high heat, melt the butter. Add the pineapple slices and cover with butter.
2. Add the pear, and then add the sugar gradually while stirring on low heat. After the fruit caramelizes, add the rum and, if desired, carefully flambé: Light the rum using a long kitchen match.
3. Add the mint, and cook to reduce the sauce for 3 minutes, then remove from the heat.
4. Serve the pineapple and pear warm with vanilla ice cream. Reserve the remaining sauce for other desserts.

Chef Thia's tip: If you don't use a strong rum it might not catch fire.

Coconut Custard Sauce

BY CHEF IRIE

This sauce is a dessert enhancer that adds moistness and flavor with Caribbean ingredients. I made it for the Rum and Raisin Bread Pudding, but the sauce could also go over a pound cake, a fruit cake, or another sweet of your choice.

Makes 2 cups

1 (13½-ounce) can coconut milk

3 egg yolks

3 tablespoons sugar

½ teaspoon grated nutmeg

½ teaspoon ground cinnamon

1 teaspoon ground ginger

¼ teaspoon salt

¼ cup dark Caribbean rum

1. Heat the coconut milk in a small pot until hot but not boiling.
2. Beat the egg yolks and sugar together for about 1 minute. Temper the eggs by adding warm coconut milk slowly while continually whisking. Whisk in the spices, salt, and rum.
3. Return the mixture to the pot over medium-low heat and continue to whisk until the sauce thickens enough to coat a spoon.
4. Serve warm.

8

Drinks

When it comes to drinks, the tag "Caribbean" implies options heavy on the fruit—with good reason. The fresh tropical fruits that grow year-round throughout the islands offer an ongoing variety of naturally refreshing beverages. We take full advantage, making creative drinks with mango, guava, passion fruit, papaya, orange, pineapple, and many others. Sometimes they're blended with citrus or water and sugar, for more of a liquid consistency. At other times, they are blended pure to become thick and creamy, similar to what Americans call smoothies. And do believe that the freshness of just-picked fruit makes all the difference!

You'll also find some vegetable drinks like cucumber, carrot, or beetroot juice, flavored with lime juice, ginger, or milk. In homes with particularly spectacular grandmas, you might even find homemade ginger beer.

In the Leeward Islands you'll find a popular bitter drink called mauby made from boiled tree bark, in much the same way soursop or guanabana bark or leaves may be boiled and drunk elsewhere in the region, primarily because they are said to be good for health. Throughout the Caribbean, there are lots of drinks made of plant roots that arise from African traditions, and then there are the somewhat unorthodox flavors like Irish moss and isinglass that men drink in the hopes of bolstering their libido.

Some drinks are flavored with sweet spices—for example, carrot juice can be enhanced with spices like cinnamon and nutmeg, especially when mixed with milk, and hot chocolate will often have cinnamon, nutmeg, and star anise added for more warmth and pungency.

Moving on to the cocktails, rum, as a byproduct of what was once the Caribbean's main export, sugar, is the most prominent alcoholic drink of Caribbean origin. You'll also find a variety of beers and liqueurs like citrus-based Blue Curaçao and coffee-based Tia Maria manufactured in the region.

In this chapter, Chef Irie and Chef Thia share their own Caribbean-inspired drink concoctions, for a wetter, and maybe happier, taste of the islands!

Carrot Juice Cocktail

BY CHEF IRIE

In Jamaica, we just call this carrot juice, but not everybody adds rum to it. This recipe is strained smooth and refined with spices, to elevate it to cocktail status. It's sweet and tangy from the apple, lime juice, and brown sugar.

Serves 4 to 6

1½ pounds carrots, roughly chopped

1 Granny Smith apple, cored and roughly chopped

2-inch piece fresh ginger

¼ cup fresh lime juice

1 teaspoon grated nutmeg

6 tablespoons brown sugar

2 tablespoons white sugar

2 to 4 ounces white rum (optional)

1. Put the carrot, apple, and 5 cups water in a blender and blend for 20 to 30 seconds. Add the ginger and blend until smooth.
2. Line a strainer or fine-mesh sieve with a cheesecloth and place over a bowl or pitcher. Pour the juice through and discard the pulp.
3. Add the lime juice, nutmeg, brown sugar, white sugar, and, if desired, rum. Stir until the sugar is completely dissolved, then place in the refrigerator to chill. Serve cold.

Papaya Cocktail

BY CHEF IRIE

I believe that you should be able to make a cocktail out of any fruit or vegetable. I wanted to try a less common fruit for this cocktail, so I chose the papaya. I added basil leaves for an earthy twist and grenadine for color and sweetness. And, of course, I use plenty of rum.

Serves 4

2 cups cubed ripe papaya

2 cups orange juice

2 tablespoons fresh lemon juice

4 tablespoons sugar

2 tablespoons grenadine

½ cup dark Caribbean rum

6 fresh basil leaves, plus more chopped basil for garnish

1. Put the papaya, orange juice, lemon juice, sugar, grenadine, rum, and basil in a blender and blend until smooth.
2. Pour over ice into chilled glasses and garnish with fresh basil.

Photograph by Nicole Hylton Richards.

Pineapple Ginger Cocktail

BY CHEF IRIE

Run away to the tropics with this sweet-and-spicy cocktail that uses whole chunks of fresh pineapple and turns the heat up a notch with sliced serrano peppers.

Serves 2 to 4

½ cup sliced fresh ginger

4 tablespoons sugar

1 serrano pepper, sliced

2 cups roughly chopped fresh pineapple

2 tablespoons fresh lime juice

1 teaspoon vanilla extract

¼ cup triple sec

1 cup rum

2 cups ice

2 to 4 teaspoons grenadine

Zest of 1 lime, cut off in strips

1. Put the ginger and 2 cups water to a blender and blend until smooth. Line a strainer or fine-mesh sieve with a cheesecloth and place over a bowl, pour the ginger juice through, and discard the pulp. Set the juice aside.

2. Add 1 teaspoon sugar and 2 to 3 slices of serrano pepper to each cocktail glass. Gently muddle the pepper and sugar and allow to sit for a few minutes.

3. Put the pineapple, lime juice, vanilla, 3 tablespoons sugar, the triple sec, and rum in a blender with the ginger juice and blend until smooth. Add the ice to the blender and blend just until the consistency is smooth and slushy.

4. Pour into the glasses and add a small splash of grenadine to the top of each cocktail.

5. Twist lime zest pieces to release the oils and run them around the rim of each glass. Drop a little zest into each glass for garnish.

Coconut Cocktail

BY CHEF IRIE

A creamy tropical cocktail made with spices for an extraordinarily mellow kick.

Serves 4

3 cups pineapple chunks, fresh or frozen

3 to 4 cups ice

1½ cups coconut milk

1 teaspoon ground ginger

1 teaspoon ground cinnamon

1 teaspoon grated nutmeg

1 teaspoon vanilla extract

1 cup white (or dark) Caribbean rum

Orange for zesting (optional)

1. Add all the ingredients except the orange zest to a blender, blend until smooth, and pour into cocktail glasses.
2. If you'd like, use a channel knife to peel off strings of orange zest, tie into knots, and drop into the glasses for garnish.

Photograph by Nicole Hylton Richards.

Special Cucumber Lemonade

BY CHEF IRIE

This is a summer drink. It's a play on the lemonade and iced tea drink called an Arnold Palmer. With pureed cucumber, simple syrup, mint, lemon, and vodka, it's a great refresher.

Serves 4

3 cucumbers

1½ cups simple syrup (equal parts sugar and water, heated to dissolve the sugar, and cooled)

½ cup fresh lemon juice

1 cup vodka

Mint leaves

1. Peel and dice the cucumbers. Put in a blender along with the simple syrup, then blend until liquefied.
2. Strain the mixture to remove solid bits, then add the lemon juice and vodka and stir.
3. Muddle mint leaves and add them with ice, then serve in chilled glasses with whole mint leaves as garnish.

A Cocktail Showdown

Singer Kevin Lyttle's 2004 megahit "Turn Me On" was, at one time, one of the most popular songs in the world. In their downtime, Kevin and his wife, Jackie, both from the island of St. Vincent, enjoy what we call "liming"—taking it easy with friends, food, drink, and music—in their backyard.

Members of the *Taste the Islands* production team happened to be great friends with his family, so the Lyttles invited our crew to shoot a segment with them. The episode quickly turned into a mixology showdown between Jackie and Chef Irie, with Kevin as the judge of the competition. During the conversation before the "drink-off," Kevin shared some thoughts on his favorite culinary spots from his travels around the world, including an

Indian food spot in Japan—go figure! He then stirred up a bit of controversy by claiming that the best Jamaican-style patties he had tasted actually came from a bakery in his native St. Vincent. Chef Irie, the Jamaican, was having none of it! And thus, the battle began.

Since Kevin most often stays away from matters of the kitchen, Jackie took up the mantle. She proceeded to make a sorrel (hibiscus) drink recipe from the menu at the couple's restaurant in St. Vincent. The cocktail included spicy ginger, brown sugar, and a splash of Vincentian rum. Chef Irie took his "food on fiyah" mantra a step further, creating a "drink on fiyah" with his Irie Shot, a sweet-hot combination of rum, mint leaves, strawberries, and jalapeños. Both drinks were

full-bodied with a tropical essence, and the crew of course got a little tipsy doing taste tests of their own.

Kevin chose his wife's drink as the winner. We're still not sure his decision was impartial, but we'll leave it for you to decide . . . ☀

Facing page, left to right: Dr. Jacqueline James-Lyttle, Kevin Lyttle, and Chef Irie. *Top, left to right*: Kevin Lyttle, Dr. Jacqueline James-Lyttle, and Chef Irie. *Bottom, left to right*: Calibe Thompson, Chef Irie, Dr. Jacqueline James-Lyttle, Kevin Lyttle, and Lukkee Chong.

The Irie Shot

BY CHEF IRIE

I made this drink up on a visit to Kevin and Jackie Lyttle's home. It's sweet and tropical, with a spicy kick from the jalapeño. I always say "food on fiyah," and this one is a drink on fiyah!

Serves 2

4 to 6 fresh mint leaves

¼ cup simple syrup (equal parts sugar and water, heated to dissolve the sugar, and cooled), plus more for the glasses

4 thin slices jalapeño pepper, plus more for garnish

1 teaspoon grated fresh ginger

2 large strawberries, sliced, plus more for garnish

1 cup dark Caribbean rum

1 cup tangerine juice

Sugar for the glasses

Strips of orange peel cut off with a channel knife (optional)

1. Smash and rub the mint leaves in your palms to release the mint oils. Put the mint leaves, simple syrup, and jalapeño in a cocktail shaker, then muddle them together. Add the ginger and strawberries and muddle again. Add the rum, tangerine juice, and ice cubes, then shake together.
2. Dip the rim of each glass into simple syrup and then sugar to coat. Add ice, and pour the cocktail over ice. Garnish with strawberry and jalapeño slices, or strips of orange peel.

Surreal

BY JACKIE JAMES-LYTTLE

Surreal (a play on the word *sorrel*) is a drink that singer Kevin Lyttle and his wife, Jackie, serve at their restaurant, Chill'n, back home on the island of St. Vincent. The recipe is close to the traditional sorrel recipe that Caribbean folks enjoy, often around Christmastime. The Lyttles' version is made special by the use of nutmeg, ginger, and an extra splash of Vincentian rum.

Serves 1

For the Sorrel Ginger Mix

1 cup dried sorrel/hibiscus

1-inch piece fresh ginger, sliced

For Each Drink

1 cup sorrel ginger mix

1 heaping teaspoon brown sugar

2 ounces dark Caribbean rum (preferably from St. Vincent)

Pinch of grated nutmeg

1. Make the sorrel ginger mix: Bring the sorrel, ginger, and 4 cups water to a boil , then turn off the heat and allow to steep overnight on the stove. Strain the cooled mixture through a cheesecloth, discarding the solid particles.
2. In a large glass jar, combine the 1 cup sorrel ginger mix with the brown sugar, rum, and nutmeg. Stir together until combined, add ice, and serve.

Chocolat Chaud (Spiced Hot Chocolate)

BY CHEF THIA

This recipe brings me back to my childhood. Back home we grate raw cocoa from the cocoa tree to make hot chocolate. Fresh raw cocoa isn't widely available in the United States and other countries, so this recipe uses a combination of milk and dark chocolate for a similar taste. It's sweet with a little spice, incorporating cinnamon, star anise, and nutmeg, just like we make back home.

My grandmother liked to add a little liquor to the hot cocoa when she made it. If you want to make it alcoholic, I recommend adding a little cocoa liqueur or coffee liqueur.

Serves 4

2 cups whole milk

1½ cups evaporated milk

2 cinnamon sticks

¼ teaspoon grated nutmeg

5 pods star anise

1 cup dark chocolate chips

1 cup semisweet chocolate chips

1 teaspoon vanilla extract

Sweetened condensed milk (optional)

1. Combine the whole milk, evaporated milk, cinnamon sticks, nutmeg, and star anise in a medium saucepan over low heat and bring to a gentle boil, stirring occasionally. Remove from the heat. Mix in the dark and semisweet chocolate chips, stirring continuously with a whisk until melted.
2. Return the pan to low heat. When the mixture begins to boil, remove it from the heat and strain through a fine-mesh sieve or a strainer lined with cheesecloth to remove the solid spices.
3. Stir in the vanilla. If desired, add condensed milk to taste.

Pineapple Ginger Simple Syrup

BY CHEF IRIE

This recipe utilizes the skin of the pineapple, offering a way to transform what would normally be considered waste. The pineapple skin is boiled, and the resulting juice is used to make a pineapple-flavored simple syrup. Allow it to cool, and then use this syrup in the Pineapple Ginger Cocktail (page 191), or try it in another cocktail.

Makes 2 cups

1- to 2-inch piece fresh ginger

1 cup fresh pineapple skin, cut into 1-inch slices

1 cup sugar

1. Combine the ginger, 1 cup water, and pineapple skin in a blender. Blend on high speed until smooth.
2. Line a strainer or fine-mesh sieve with a cheesecloth and place over a bowl or pitcher. Pour the liquid through and discard the pulp. Measure out 1 cup of the liquid and set aside.
3. In a medium saucepan, dissolve the sugar in 1 cup water and bring to a boil, about 3 to 5 minutes. Remove from the heat and allow to cool.
4. When the simple syrup has cooled, add the pineapple and ginger liquid to the syrup and stir to combine. Store unused syrup in a clean glass jar in the refrigerator for up to 3 days.

Haitian Rum Punch

BY CHEF THIA

This is my version of classic Haitian rum punch. Fruity and a little tart, this rum punch is more like a blended slushie cocktail. I use Haitian rum, of course, for the most authentic taste. Frozen passion fruit puree gives the punch a tart, tropical flavor, and grenadine, fruit punch, and brown sugar give it plenty of sweetness.

Serves 4

2 cups frozen passion fruit puree

¼ cup Haitian rum

1½ cups fruit punch

½ cup white rum

2 to 3 tablespoons grenadine

1½ tablespoons brown sugar

1. Combine the passion fruit puree and rum in a food processor. Add the fruit punch, rum, grenadine, and brown sugar and blend until smooth.
2. Serve in cocktail glasses.

Calibe Thompson, Adam Heim, Chef Irie, Brandon Mitchell, Ben Clerveaux, and Tyler Council (*top row, left to right*); Rory Lee, Lisa Lee Arneaud, and Lukkee Chong (*bottom row, left to right*).

Acknowledgments

This book is made possible by a team of people who have a passion for life, friendship, and good food. There are a number of people and entities we want to thank collectively, as well as some from our personal lives that we want to thank individually.

To our production team, who made things work in challenging circumstances, and for bonuses including hugs and leftovers, we appreciate you so much. Associate producer Lukkee Chong, director of photography Adam Heim, editor Katie Hidden, camera operators including Tyler and Jonathan, our trusty hair and makeup team of Rory Lee, our facilitators Allison Hunte, Tyrone Robertson, and Maria and Bella Foxhall, and everyone else who lent a hand pulling everything together, thank you.

To our non-chef hosts Nicole Hylton-Richards, who was a trooper from the start and often performed double duty as our photographer, and Lisa Lee Arneaud, who always brought the cheer and chatter, thank you. To our guests including Ato Boldon, Maxi Priest, Kevin and Jackie Lyttle, the members of the Inner Circle band, Franz Hall, Alison Hinds, and Rory Lee, thank you for the stories and the memories.

To David and Angelique Walters, who allowed us to commandeer their home for our production purposes, as did Allison, we know we couldn't have done it without you.

We have to thank Paul Pennicook and the team from Jamaica, Billy, Seymour, Grace, Robert, and the team from Barbados Tourism Marketing Inc., Derrick and Grace Foods, and Christopher and Lakay Food, without whom we wouldn't have made it on the air.

To David I. Muir, who took the majority of the beautiful photos in this book, thank you from all of us.

From South Florida PBS we'd like to thank Dolores Sukhdeo, Jeff Huff, Frances Hernandez, Max Duke, and Joyce Belloise. From American Public Television, for helping us to navigate the waters, we'd like to thank Colette Greenstein and Dawn Anderson. Our attorneys Levi Williams and Marlon Hill were also an invaluable help.

To our helpers and tasters, including Chef Vicky and Tommy Colas, Michael Sims, and Kairo Muir, we thank you!

Chef Irie's Personal Thank-Yous

I'll keep it simple. I'd like to thank my mom, Mrs. Maudlyn Sinclair, my sisters Pauline Whittingham Jackson and Sandra Whittingham, my brother Ralston Whittingham, and the rest of my family. For always supporting me, I'd like to thank Marcia Narine, Karen Grey, Donovan Terrelonge and Mayra Solomon, Karen McGibbons, Chef Wayne Bryan (RIP), Ernisha Randolph, Chef Albert Charles, my UF (University of Florida) crew, David & Angelique Walters, June Minto, Treisha Hall, Chef Allan Lazar, Chef Patricia Wilson, Nouchelle and Oliver Hastings, Devand Sukhdeo, Boatyard (formerly Bimini Boatyard), Shuck-n-Dive restaurant, Adache Architects, and Bermello, Ajamil & Partners.

Chef Thia's Personal Thank-Yous

Thank you to God!

I want to thank my children. Without them my world would have been so empty. Alexandre Verna (my bino, my strength), Thaïs Elie (Thayou, my love), and Enya Germain (ma mouch-mouch, mon bebe). To my amazing parents Denise Mangones—ma maman cherie, Jacky Verna—mon papa d'amour, Florence Verna (my second mom), Suzanne Mangones (Grandma, Mamie Suzanne), my loving baby brother Jean-Pierre Verna, my wonderful baby sister Anne Marie Suzanne Verna (my ninouche Annie), my beautiful sister-in-law Dr. Lisa Verna, Ludwigh Aarestrup, and Hantz Bennett (brother) and family.

To my best friend no longer with me, Olivier Cardozo, to my ex-husband Pierre-Richard Elie, who pushed me to pursue my dreams, to Kristine and Rudy Larose—a lifetime of pure friendship. Thank you to Carolle Larose, Chantal Bouchereau, Carl Christian, (Chef Vicky) Vicky Colas and Tommy Gilbert, attorney Sabine Millien-Felix, Dr. Joelle Balmir-Thevenin, Regine Milford, Jean-Pierre Blanchard, my aunt I miss so much Gysandre Blanchard, Tatie Grish Ingrid Roy, Cybel (Ma Poulette) B. Boyer, Joel Blanchard, Saskya Blanchard Vaval (Saskitouche), Martine Jeanty, Nastassia Roy D'Meza (Ma Nanou), Patricia Mangones Polas, Jonathan J. Perry, Saskya Sky, Donald Guerrie, Carel Pedre, Samuel Dameus, Richard Lecoin, Patricia Desamours, Jimmy Moise, Samantha Raymond, Gary Métayer, Joseph Nicolas (Chef Joe), Sandra Florvella, Genevieve Blanchard (Tatie Ginou), Ansy (my amazing neighbor), Se Marie, Frantz Prospere, Marjorie Germain, Ketsia Elie, Douglas Elie, Jenny Adrien, Calibe Thompson, David Muir, Deborah Vaval, Carline Phanor, Christopher Dupuy, Gilbert and Tayma Nau, Naomi Acra, Jovana Louis Benoit, Carl and Melissa Apollon, Jean-Marc Schomberg, Marie-Claude Nelson, Kursteen Nelson Champagne (Tita), Fabienne Alphonse-Reid, Tatiana Elie, Didier Fabien, Gladys Lavaud, Dr. Pierre-Richard Limousin, Karoll-Ann Fanfan, Ambassador Paul Altidor, Neïma Bélancourt-Herraux, Chef Shorne Benjamin, Pierre Garçon, and finally to the woman who never stopped believing in me, who raised me, but who is no longer with me—this book I dedicate it to you, ma Mamie Annie. I love you so very much and miss you terribly.

With all my heart I thank and love you all for the love and support.

Calibe's Personal Thank-Yous

I would like to thank the entire team including these two crazy chefs whom I always either want to hug or spank, sometimes simultaneously. I'd also like to thank my family, who have been as supportive as they could, through rough patches and good ones, especially my mommy Clover. Thanks to Clinton, Camille, Carol, Chantal, Chandelle, Mateo, Nicholas, Aunt Ina, and Melissa. And to everyone who has supported and cheered us on through this whirlwind journey. Bless you, and thank you!

Producer's Message

When we started on the pilot for *Taste the Islands with Chef Irie* in 2013, we had no idea where it would go. My intention was national television, but we didn't know how to get there. Irie was excited to star in his own show, and I was excited to create something of the caliber I thought would be worthy of a mainstream audience. I had no money, so I sold my 2007 Toyota Corolla for some seed capital and borrowed a friend's bicycle for transportation. I asked a friend, Allison, if we could shoot in her kitchen, and I lobbied some recent graduates of film school whose work I respected and who showed some respect for our teeny tiny-budget. It was a tight ship, and I edited every frame of that first season with my own two hands. It sat on my computer for almost a year, until Irie shared that he knew someone at our local PBS station. I reached out to her, and we made it through the door because the team at the station liked Irie as a chef. When they saw the work we had done together, they liked that, too! The remainder of the journey to national broadcast was a challenging climb, but a very gratifying one. There were tears when we hit our funding goals, tears when we heard the level of pickup we received from stations around the country, and tears when we heard that Create TV wanted the show.

People are always surprised to learn that I'm not a foodie. I do love to learn about food, but I'm not particularly a fan of eating anything exotic nor cooking anything at all. But there's a passion that goes into the work of those who do love to cook that I find beautiful. I feel like they have that certain sense of joy people find when they are truly connected to something. When Caribbean folks cook, they often won't be satisfied unless the people eating are. I've almost been thrown out of friends' houses because I showed up and wasn't hungry!

Working on *Taste the Islands*, learning with the chefs as they researched the traditional dishes of Caribbean countries they *weren't* born in, and then seeing how they would interpret those dishes, has brought me a different level of joy. The simple understanding of cultural and regional food origins, spices and flavors, and seeing how ingredients (like plantains, cornmeal, or rice) are used in one country versus another, has been fascinating. I hope we've done a good job of translating all our discovery and curiosity onto television screens and into this book.

Two television seasons later, we've grown our suite of offerings and plan to keep growing. Since working on the TV show, we've created two cookbooks in the *Taste the Islands Essentials* series called *50 Favorite Jamaican Recipes* and *50 Favorite Haitian Recipes*; we've launched an annual culinary festival called the Taste the Islands Experience, where Thia and Irie are resident chefs; and we've created a traveling exhibit called the Taste the Islands Caribbean Culinary Museum and Theater with historical information, artifacts, and dramatic presentations of food history we've learned about along the way. This book represents the tying together of all that the chefs have made and the team has experienced in the making of *Taste the Islands*. I'm grateful to all involved for helping us to make it happen.

Calibe

Substitutions

Boniatos	not available
Browning sauce	mushroom soy sauce
Calabaza	butternut squash, kabocha squash
Chayote squash	green Anjou pears
Chorizo	andouille sausage
Cilantro	parsley or herb of choice
Coconut milk	almond milk
Culantro	omit or use herb of choice
***Djon-djon* mushrooms**	squid ink
Guava pulp	guava paste, quince paste
Jicama	Bosc pear
Key lime	lime or other tart citrus
Malanga	not available
Marjoram	oregano
Passion fruit puree	tamarind paste, mango puree, or unsweetened applesauce
Phyllo dough	lumpia or wonton skins
Salted codfish/bacalao	any other salted white fish
Star anise pod	1 inch black licorice root
Sugarcane juice	agave nectar
Tangerine juice	orange juice
Yellow yam	not available

Glossary

Adobo A meat or poultry seasoning that includes salt, pepper, garlic, oregano, olive oil, and vinegar.

Anaheim pepper Long, green, narrow chile with a low heat factor, used often in Southwest cuisines.

Avocado A light green to dark purple-skinned fruit, roughly the shape of a pear, with creamy, light green flesh.

Bay leaves Leaves of the laurel tree, used as a seasoning in dishes for their herbal, slightly floral aroma, similar to oregano or thyme. Bay leaves should always be removed from the pot before serving your dish.

Black beans Called *frijoles negros* in Latin-Caribbean cuisine where they are most commonly used, these small, black, kidney-shaped beans have a smoky, mushroom-like flavor.

Calabaza A pumpkin-like squash, popular throughout the Caribbean and Central and South America. Also called West Indian pumpkin. You can substitute butternut squash.

Cassava Also called yuca, the cassava is a starchy root that has tough brown skin and crisp, neutral-flavored white flesh.

Chayote squash Also called cho-cho, mirliton, or christophine, this pear-shaped gourd with pale green skin can be boiled, sautéed, baked, stuffed, or consumed raw in salads.

Cilantro A pungent, flat-leaf herb resembling parsley. The flavor is strong and sweet, with a citrus scent. Parsley may be substituted, but it has a much less distinctive taste.

Cloves Dried cloves are an aromatic spice used to flavor meats, curries, marinades, spice blends, and even hot beverages.

Coconut milk A liquid extracted from shredded, dried coconut meat by soaking it with water, pressing, and straining. It is available canned.

Coriander The seed of the cilantro plant.

Culantro An herb from the parsley family, with long leaves and a strong, earthy taste.

Cumin A seed used as a spice, whole or ground, for its distinctive flavor and earthy, warming and aromatic character. It is a staple in certain stews, soups, curry, chili, and some pickles and pastries.

Flat-leaf parsley A variety of parsley with large leaves and a more pungent flavor than curly parsley.

Jicama A bulbous root vegetable with a taste similar to a very mild and slightly sweet radish. Jicama is crisp and white with thick brown skin. Use raw or slightly cooked as a vegetable.

Kosher salt Also known as coarse or pickling salt, kosher salt is pure, refined rock salt. It is larger and has a milder taste than table salt. Use kosher salt when specified in the recipes; otherwise use sea salt.

Malanga A vegetable closely related to the taro root, also called coco yam. It is similar in shape to a white potato.

Mango A tropical fruit with smooth yellow to red skin, and sweet, orange-yellow flesh, tender to the touch. The skin should be peeled, the pit removed, and the flesh alone should be eaten.

Papaya A mild-flavored fruit with orange or green skin, and bright orange or pink flesh. It is tender to the touch and shaped like an elongated pear.

Serrano pepper These peppers are bright green and are typically eaten raw. They are significantly hotter than jalapeño peppers and are commonly used in making sauces like pico de gallo and salsa.

The three authors (*left to right*), Chef Thia, Chef Irie, and Calibe Thompson.

About the Authors

Hugh Sinclair

Jamaican-born Hugh A. Sinclair is better known as "Chef Irie," a jovial television personality and professionally trained private chef and caterer specializing in elegant, Caribbean-inspired cuisine. His flavor-curious mind has developed an approach to cuisine that fuses the culinary influence of the Caribbean, where he grew up, with the influence of his travels through Europe and the Far East.

Since 2015, he has been the lead personality on the Caribbean cooking and travel series *Taste the Islands*, which airs nationwide on public television in the United States. He also appeared in an episode of the Food Network show *Cutthroat Kitchen*. In 2018, Sinclair was the host chef for the Savoring Jamaica team at the James Beard House and a guest chef of Team Jamaica at the Caribbean Holidays Guest Chef Series in the Delegates Dining Room at the United Nations. He has been a featured chef at the South Beach Wine and Food Festival, and has been invited to international events including Gout et Saveurs Lakay in Haiti and Bayfest in St Lucia. He's even been invited to be a guest chef on Holland America cruise line. Sinclair has worked at some of South Florida's premier establishments including Turnberry Isle Resort and Bimini Boatyard. Never one to stray far from his roots, you can find him every year hosting the culinary stages as the resident chef at the Grace Jamaican Jerk Festivals in New York; Washington, DC; and Florida.

As a child, his home was on a sugarcane plantation called Caymanas Estates in the parish of St. Catherine, Jamaica. His father, Girvan, was a bookkeeper there, and his mother, Maudlyn, was a homemaker and entrepreneur. He and his cousins would play in the hills and canefields, enjoying local food and sneaking sips of rum.

After high school, he moved to the United States, where he earned a bachelor of arts degree in architecture from the University of Florida in Gainesville, before switching focus to earn a degree in culinary arts from Johnson & Wales University in North Miami. Today, his television and live audiences, across the United States and internationally, enjoy his palpable love of learning and sharing knowledge about the wonders of delicious island food.

Cynthia Verna

With a smile often described as blinding, Haitian-born Cynthia "Chef Thia" Verna has a larger-than-life personality that lights up a room. She is a personal chef, accomplished author, and cooking show host who specializes in gourmet Caribbean-fusion cuisine.

Verna is known for incorporating Caribbean, African, Latin, Asian, French, and Mediterranean flavors into her fine-dining repertoire. Her professional culinary life started in her mother's restaurant in Haiti when she was seventeen years old. Not long after, she opened her own restaurant—Atelier Les Bamboos. She studied under top Haitian chef Reginald Koury and worked at the prestigious Club Med kitchen before moving to the United States at the age of twenty-one.

She went on to graduate cum laude from Le Cordon Bleu culinary institute in her new home of Miami, Florida. She has been affiliated with two Ritz-Carlton franchises, and has been a culinary representative for Haitian consulates, presenting at events in Italy, Suriname, Taiwan, and Vietnam.

In May 2017 she became the first woman to win the People's Choice award at the Embassy Chef Challenge in Washington, DC, representing Haiti and beating master chefs from more than thirty other countries. She's also been given one of North Miami's highest distinctions. For her accomplishments in the culinary arts, the city presented a proclamation naming November 18, 2017, "Cynthia Verna Day."

She made her debut as co-host of *Taste the Islands* in June 2017 when the second season of the Caribbean cooking series premiered nationwide on Create TV. In collaboration with the show's creators, she co-authored her first cookbook, *50 Favorite Haitian Recipes*.

As a renowned social media tastemaker, Verna's live videos have garnered tens of thousands of views. She is a survivor of sexual assault who has become a sought-after public figure, with much of her messaging involving spiritual inspiration and self-motivation. She is a mother of three, living and working as a culinary professional in South Florida.

Calibe Thompson

Calibe Thompson is the creator and executive producer of *Taste the Islands* and the head dread at Blondie Ras Productions, the company behind the television and cookbook series. She is also the creative director at Island Syndicate, which produces the Taste the Islands Experience culinary event series. She is an outgoing Jamaican American entrepreneur with titles including TV producer, magazine and book publisher, director, host, best-selling author, columnist, and public speaker.

In 2015, she became the first Jamaican producer to secure series placement on national U.S. public television. Her flagship show, *Taste the Islands*, was the first Caribbean-themed culinary series that the network giants PBS and Create TV had aired throughout the United States. Her programs have been broadcast in more than forty states, more than twenty Caribbean countries, Canada, the United Kingdom, and Brunei.

She holds a bachelor of arts in architecture from the University of Technology, Jamaica, and remains married to her work. Thompson's ongoing mission is to create exceptional Caribbean-inspired content and experiences for sophisticated mainstream audiences.

Index